THE VIKING WORLD

Philippa Wingate
Dr Anne Millard BA, Ph.D.
Illustrated by Gerald Wood
Designed by Andrew Dixon

Series editor Jane Chisholm

Additional illustrations by **Dan Courtney** and **Kevin Lyles**

Additional designs by **Sharon Bennet** and **Rebecca Halverson**

Map illustrations by **Peter Dennis**

With thanks to **Lynn Bresler** and **John Russell**

Contents

Introduction

Toward the end of the 8th century, bands of ferocious Scandinavian sea raiders, known as Vikings, began to terrorize the people of Europe. *The Viking World* studies the Vikings, describing their homes, their lives, their customs and beliefs. It explores the places they plundered and colonized, and the civilizations they came into contact with.

This book examines the period known as the Viking Age, which started in about 790 and ended in about 1100. It began with the Vikings' first raids in Europe, and came to a close when their aggressive military expeditions ended and the people of Scandinavia settled down to a more peaceful way of life.

How we know about the Vikings

Every year archaeologists make exciting discoveries which add to our knowledge of the Vikings. The information we have is gathered from a variety of sources.

By studying the remains of Viking trading towns, houses and craftsmen's workshops, we can find out about their building methods and the tools they used.

In Viking culture it was customary to bury people with their personal possessions. Weapons, furniture, jewels and clothing have been found in graves. These objects can tell us about the Vikings' daily lives. Objects which come from foreign lands show us the routes of Viking travels and where they raided and traded.

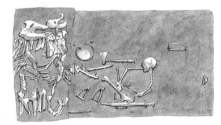

This picture shows the remains of a Viking surrounded by his grave goods.

Archaeological finds have provided valuable information about how Viking ships were built and sailed. Well preserved ships have been found in burial mounds and five ships were excavated in Denmark, where they had been sunk to block a narrow fjord.

Much of our information about the Vikings comes from accounts written by people who came into contact with them. Some were the victims of Viking raids; others were Arabs or Christians, who did not worship the Vikings' gods. The authors of these accounts are likely, therefore, to have been biased against the men from the north.

A 13th century manuscript showing a Viking king

The Vikings told tales of their exploits. A few stories, called sagas, have survived, passed down by word of mouth for centuries before being written down in the 13th century by Christian scholars. Their writings give an insight into the character of the Vikings and their spirit of adventure.

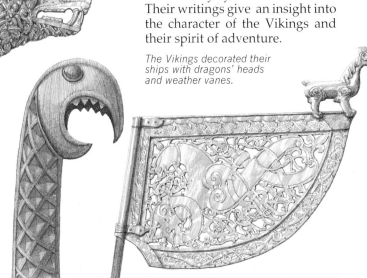

The Vikings decorated their ships with dragons' heads and weather vanes.

Dates

If historians are unsure exactly when an event occurred, the date is shown with a "c" in front of it. This stands for *circa*, the Latin for "about".

There are a few events in this book that precede the birth of Jesus Christ. These are indicated by the letters B.C., which stand for 'Before Christ'.

The language of the Vikings

People who lived in Scandinavia during the Viking Age spoke a language which today we call Old Norse. Experts think that people living in the areas now known as Norway, Denmark and Sweden spoke very similar versions of this language and that they could therefore understand each other without difficulty.

Unfamiliar words

Words printed in italic type, like *Thing*, are Viking words. Some of the more difficult words in this book are followed by a star (*). These and other words associated with the Vikings are explained in the glossary. You can read more about the most important people who lived during the time of the Vikings in the "Who was who".

Who were the Vikings?

People who lived in Scandinavia between about 750 and 1100 are known as Vikings. At first they were farmers, craftsmen and merchants. By the 9th century, they turned to piracy and plundering, terrorizing the people of Western Europe. Later, many of them became settlers, leaving the shores of Scandinavia to find new lands to colonize and farm. The Vikings acquired a reputation as brave and ruthless warriors, but they were also skilled craftsmen who created beautiful treasures and artifacts.

Europe before the Viking Age

In the 5th and 6th centuries, Europe was in turmoil. The chaos began when a tribe called the Huns, left their homeland in the Steppes (plains which stretch from Mongolia to eastern Europe) and migrated west across Asia into eastern and central Europe. Their arrival forced other tribes, Goths, Jutes, Burgundians, Vandals, Angles, Franks and Saxons, to leave their homes in northern and eastern Europe and retreat westward.

In doing so, they seized lands that had belonged to the Roman empire, before it collapsed in the 5th century

In both the 7th and 10th centuries, eastern and south-eastern Europe was invaded by a new wave of immigrants from the Steppes. These included people called Patzinaks, Slavs, Avars, Bulgars and Magyars.

Nomadic horsemen

Scandinavia before the Vikings

Scandinavia escaped invasion both by the Romans and the barbarian tribes who overran Roman territories. Left in peace, Scandinavian culture thrived.

Archaeological evidence shows that before the 9th century, the people of Scandinavia were farmers and merchants. They established very profitable trading links with the Roman Empire and with the many kingdoms set up after its fall. This period of prosperity in Scandinavia is known as the "Age of Gold". Graves of chieftains of that period have been found filled with rich and exquisite treasure.

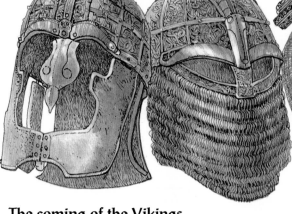

An early chieftain on horseback

These helmets were made before the Viking Age.

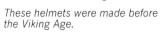

A gold necklace and a sword hilt inlaid with gold panels

The coming of the Vikings

As the 8th century came to an end, Scandinavia was prospering. Experts believe that this prosperity led to an increase in population. The area's limited agricultural land was unable to support the growing number of people. So as a result, Scandinavians began to raid nearby lands, returning home with their ships loaded with looted treasure and slaves. Raiders from both Denmark and Norway sailed west. They attacked England and mainland Europe and explored the Atlantic for new land to settle. Swedish warriors sailed east instead, crossing the Baltic into eastern Europe and beyond.

Not all Vikings were murderous pirates or settlers. Many stayed at home, living and working in peace.

This stone carving from England shows Viking raiders armed with axes.

The geography of Scandinavia

The Vikings came from areas in Scandinavia that are now the countries Denmark, Norway and Sweden. Scandinavia is today, as it was in Viking times, a place of great contrasts in both geography and climate.

Denmark

Denmark enjoys the mildest climate of all the Scandinavian countries. The terrain is very flat and there are extensive areas of rich farmland along the Danish coast and on its islands. This is interspersed with dense woods, heaths and sand dunes.

Denmark is a much smaller country than Norway or Sweden. Most of it is located on a peninsula that is joined to mainland Europe. In Viking times, the southern tip of modern Sweden was also part of Danish territory.

Denmark includes approximately 600 islands, and many have very fertile soil.

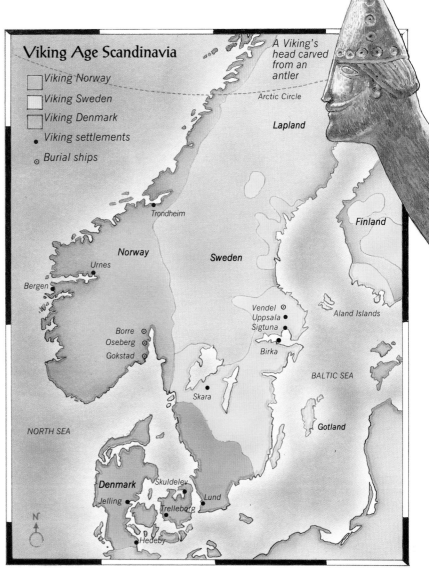

Viking Age Scandinavia

☐ Viking Norway
☐ Viking Sweden
☐ Viking Denmark
• Viking settlements
◎ Burial ships

A Viking's head carved from an antler

Arctic Circle

Lapland

Finland

Trondheim

Norway

Sweden

Urnes

Bergen

Vendel ◎
Uppsala •
Sigtuna •

Aland Islands

Borre ◎
Oseberg ◎
Gokstad ◎

Birka

BALTIC SEA

Skara

NORTH SEA

Gotland

Denmark   Skuldelev

Jelling •   Lund

Trelleborg

N

Hedeby

Sweden

During the Viking Age, most of the settlements in Sweden were situated in the southern part of the country, particularly on the shores of lakes and near the Baltic coast, where soils were fertile.

The land in the north is mountainous and forested, and weather conditions are harsh. Parts of both Sweden and Norway lie within the Arctic Circle, where in winter it is dark both day and night.

Snow covered mountains and forests under the light of the midnight sun.

Norway

Norway is a very mountainous country. Its 2,000 mile long coastline has thousands of long, narrow inlets, called "fjords", which are bordered by rocks and mountains. The majority of Viking settlements in Norway were situated on the rich soils found on the edges of these fjords and along the country's river valleys.

A farm at the side of a steep-sided, rocky fjord on the coast of Norway.

What does "Viking" mean?

Experts disagree about the meaning of the word "Viking". Some think it originates from the word *vik*, which comes from Old Norse, the language of the Vikings. *Vik* means a "bay" or "creek", so that "*Viking*" would have applied to someone who kept his ship in a bay. Others think it comes from the word *vikingr*, which means "pirate" or "raider". The Scandinavian expression "to go *a-Viking*" meant to go on an expedition in search of wealth and glory.

Life on a Viking farm

Most Vikings lived by farming. In areas where soils were good, small farming communities grew up, producing a variety of crops and animals. The population in these areas increased rapidly and soon there were too many people to be supported by the land.

Some families were forced to cultivate isolated areas where the soil was thin. Poor soil increased the risk of crops failing during a bad season. This could mean that a farmer and his family starved during the long winter months. As a result, many people were driven overseas to find new agricultural land to settle on and farm.

Working on the farm

Viking farms had to be largely self-sufficient, people produced their own food, cloth, leather goods and tools. Most farmers owned their own farms and ran them with the help of their families. Others paid landless men and women to perform skilled tasks, such as planting crops, or working as a carpenter, a blacksmith or as a cooper, making barrels for storage. Wealthy landowners had slaves to fetch and carry, spread manure on the fields, chop wood and dig up rotted vegetable matter, called peat, which was used as fuel.

*A farm worker sowing seeds, pictured in the Bayeux Tapestry**

During the spring, farmers began preparing their land for planting crops. In summer, there was less to do on the farm, so men often went on raiding or hunting expeditions. When autumn came, farmers would harvest crops and stock up food for the winter. In winter, some farmers went hunting to bring home extra food and furs.

Longhouse

Enclosure for animals

Wood store

Blacksmith's forge

Grass and hay provided fodder and bedding for animals.

Pigs

Chickens and geese

Food store – In autumn, the weakest animals were slaughtered. Meat and fish were salted, dried in the sun or smoked over fires to preserve them. This food fed the farmer and his household throughout the winter.

Vegetable gardens

A stream supplied fresh drinking water and a place to wash clothes.

Oats, barley, rye and wheat were planted in the fields.

A simple machine called an ard was used to cut through light soils.

Food and cooking

The most common food eaten by Vikings was fish, porridge made from oats and barley mixed with milk or water, and barley bread. Herbs and spices were used to season food, and sea salt was used for preserving meat and fish.

The Vikings drank beer made from barley and hops, and mead made from honey, water and yeast.

Wealthy people could afford to eat wheat bread, which was considered a luxury. They drank wine made from grapes imported from France and Italy.

This picture shows the buildings, crops and animals found on a Viking farm.

Horses

Sheep and goats

In summer, herders took cattle to graze on rich mountain pastures.

Workers used spades, hoes, scythes, sickles and rakes.

This picture shows the type of food Viking women prepared.

Cows' and goats' milk were used to make cheese and butter.

Meat and fish were grilled on spits and forks.

Knife and plate

Wooden bowls

Drinking horns

Grain was ground by hand between two stones to make flour.

Trough for kneading dough

Wooden ladle

Vegetables

Honey

Fruit and nuts

Eggs

Fishing and hunting

Vikings ate a lot of fish. There were many varieties in the sea and rivers, including herring, salmon and cod. Fishermen caught them with traps, nets and spears. In coastal areas, people hunted seals and walruses with spears. Whales were driven into shallow creeks, or on to beaches, where they were killed with spears by men in small boats.

Hunting was a good source of food, as well as furs and hides. Groups of men went on long hunting trips during the winter when food stocks had run low. Their prey included deer, boars, bears and smaller game, such as foxes and otters. They killed the animals with spears, bows and arrows or caught them with traps.

Men climbed down cliffs to catch sea birds, and to collect feathers which were used as padding in warm quilts and cloaks.

Inside a Viking house

Most Vikings lived in rectangular buildings consisting of one long room, called a hall, in which everyone ate, slept and worked together. In winter, many people had to share their house with farm animals, which were kept in an enclosure at one end of the room.

Chieftains and wealthy townspeople had one or two separate rooms where they could have some privacy away from other members of their family and the servants.

Different types of Viking house

The style of a Viking house depended on the climate and the materials available in the area in which it was built. In areas of Scandinavia where wood was plentiful, houses were constructed from wooden frames covered with planks. Poorer people made the walls of their houses with wattle and daub*. Roofs were usually thatched with straw or reeds, or covered with wooden tiles.

Some Viking houses had slightly curved walls, like the one below.

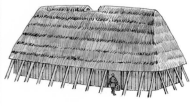

In areas where the climate was cold, like Greenland or Iceland, wood was scarce. The people there used stone and turf to build the walls of their homes.

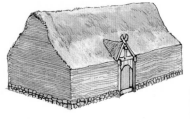

This house is made of stone and turf.

This is a cut-away picture of a chieftain's house.

Animals lived behind a partition at the back of the house.

Toilet

Storehouse

People used wooden skis or skates made of bone.

Cooking pot

Storage barrels

Metal lamp holder

A carved wooden wagon like this one was found on the Oseberg burial ship (see page 23).

People attached iron spikes to their shoes to help them cross ice or snow.

Inside a hall

Viking houses were between 15 and 30 m (50-100 ft) long. In the middle of the hall was a stone-lined hearth. A fire was used for cooking and heating and its smoke escaped through a hole in the roof. This meant the hall was often smoky and smelly.

The Vikings did not have windows with glass in them. Some houses had small openings in the walls which were covered with shutters at night. The hall would have been quite dark inside.

Oil lamps and candles were the only source of light, apart from the fire.

The floor of the hall was made of hard-packed earth, strewn with reeds or straw. There were long, wooden platforms along each side. At night, people slept on them, using pillows and quilts filled with feathers or down, and blankets and furs to keep warm.

Clothes and weapons were hung from pegs, or propped up against the walls. Valuables, clothes and bedding were kept in large chests and caskets.

A wealthy man's hall (like the one shown here) would be richly decorated. The wooden posts supporting the frame of the house were ornately carved. Tapestries made of wool hung from the walls, as decoration and to prevent draughts. These hangings could be strung between rafters to provide some privacy.

Furniture

There was little furniture in Viking houses because space was limited. Every household had a loom for making cloth. People sat on stools or on platforms around the edge of the hall. Tables were used as eating and working surfaces. The master of the house might have had a chair and a bed to sleep in.

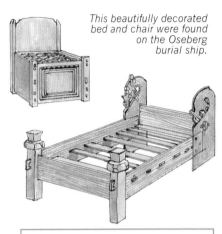

This beautifully decorated bed and chair were found on the Oseberg burial ship.

Leisure

Wrestling was a popular sport. Warriors spent their free time perfecting fighting techniques, repairing broken weapons or decorating new ones.

Inside, during long winter evenings, some people carved ornaments out of ivory or wood. Others made objects, such as pieces for board games, from wood or clay.

These chess pieces, carved from ivory, were found in the Hebrides, where Vikings settled.

Carved roof support

Tapestries

Roof covered with thatch

Walls made from planks of wood

Bed

Loom

Large wooden chests

Sledge

What the Vikings wore

Fashions in Scandinavia changed very little during the Viking Age. Most people wore clothes made of wool and linen, woven at home and dyed with vegetables and minerals.

The quality and design of a person's clothing and jewellery depended on their wealth and status. Rich people could afford garments made of fine cloth, dyed in rich shades. For feasts and special occasions they had outfits decorated with silk from China and gold and silver threads. Poor people wore plain garments, made of coarse, undyed cloth.

Women's clothes

Viking women wore long dresses, which they fastened around the neck with a drawstring or a tiny brooch. Over the dresses, they wore tunics made of wool or linen, that were often decorated with woven bands of patterned material. The tunics consisted of two rectangular pieces of cloth joined at the shoulder by straps. The straps were fastened to the tunic with a pair of brooches. Some women wore chains hanging from one of their tunic brooches, to which they attached a variety of personal items, such as a knife, a comb, keys or scissors.

Archaeologists have not found belt buckles in women's graves. They think that women tied their tunics at the waist with pieces of cloth or allowed them to hang loosely. But one saga (a Viking story) tells of a lady whose dress was taken in at the waist to show off her handsome figure.

Outside, women wore shawls, fastened around their shoulders with brooches. Some wore cloaks lined or quilted with feathers when the weather was very cold.

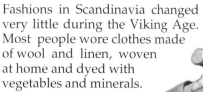

A selection of the clothes Vikings wore

A leather skull cap

A tunic made of wool

A headscarf

Shawl made of wool

Tweezers and a comb

Tunic dress

An amulet*

Tunic brooches

The dresses women wore under their tunics had long or short sleeves. This lady's dress is finely pleated.

Men's clothes

Viking men dressed in linen shirts and trousers made of wool. Their trousers were fastened around the waist with a drawstring and their trouser legs were either left straight or bound with pieces of cloth.

Over their shirts and trousers, men wore long-sleeved tunics. These were sometimes decorated at the cuffs, hem and neckline with bright, woven bands of patterned cloth. Around their tunics, men wore leather belts, from which they hung a purse or a knife.

In winter, Viking men wore furs or heavy cloaks. They kept their sword arms free by pinning their cloaks over one shoulder with cloak pins.

Both men and women wore leather shoes and boots, which fastened around their ankles.

This is a wealthy man with richly decorated clothes of fine cloth.

Cloak pinned on one shoulder

Hair styles

Viking women grew their hair very long. They wore it braided or tied in a knot on top of their heads. They tied decorative bands around their foreheads. Once married, women covered their hair with a headscarf.

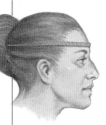

Most men had shoulder-length hair, though a few warriors grew it even longer. Some men braided the hair each side of their faces to keep it out of their eyes. Others held their hair in place with a band tied around the forehead.

Many Viking men grew beards. It was fashionable for a man to braid his beard to stop it from blowing into his face while he was hunting or fighting. Some men arranged their beards in a fork shape.

Jewellery

Viking men and women wore a lot of jewellery. Many exquisitely decorated pieces have been found in graves. Rich people could buy jewellery individually crafted from gold and silver. The less wealthy could only afford pieces of bronze, copper and iron, made in a cast.

The most popular ornaments worn by women were tunic brooches. These were usually oval-shaped and intricately patterned with stylized animals or spirals. Some were round and were gilded or decorated with silver wire. Women often wore beads strung between their tunic brooches.

Both men and women wore gold, silver and copper rings on their fingers and arms. Around their necks they wore heavy rings called torques.

A selection of Viking jewellery

A pair of brooches held a woman's tunic in place

A brooch with two arms

A richly decorated cloak pin

This buckle, from Denmark, is decorated with animals and a man's face.

A necklace made with silver coins

Gold plaques have been attached to this necklace.

Beads were made of pottery, glass, crystal, carnelian or amber (fossilized resin).

An intricate gold necklace

These gold and silver arm rings were found in Denmark.

The evidence

Pictures carved on stone monuments and scenes embroidered on tapestries give us an idea of what the Vikings wore. Some Norse stories give details about fashions and styles. The clothes normally decayed very rapidly, but pieces of cloth and items of clothing have survived, preserved in bogs or burial mounds. These have provided experts with very useful information.

This pendant, from Sweden, shows a woman in a cloak and patterned tunic, wearing beads strung between her tunic brooches.

Viking ships

The Vikings were highly skilled shipbuilders and produced some of the finest ships of their time. They gave their ships names such as *Long Serpent*, *Sea Bird*, *Wave Walker* and *Raven of the Wind*. They even wrote poems about them and carved pictures of them on stones.

Ships were essential to the Vikings' way of life. They built vessels of many different shapes and sizes. Warships and merchant ships enabled men to raid foreign lands, and allowed settlers and explorers to cross seas in search of new land and riches.

At home, the Vikings used fishing boats, ferries and canoes. Mountains, dense forests, bogs and deep snow made land travel difficult in Viking times. The many rivers, lakes and inland waterways in Scandinavia meant that travel by water was the easiest option.

This picture shows some of the main features of a Viking longship.

Longships

The most famous Viking ships are their spectacular warships known as "longships" or "dragon ships". They were long, slender vessels, swift, strong and light enough to row or even carry when necessary. The ships were designed to sail up shallow rivers or land on sloping beaches when the Vikings wanted to make surprise attacks.

Longships were usually made of oak and were about 18 m (61 ft) long and 2.6 m (8.5 ft) wide. The largest known vessel was 28 m (95 ft) long and 4.5 m (15 ft) wide. The number of oars varied from 26 to 70. They were arranged down both sides of the ship.

A large oar on the right hand side at the stern of the ship was used for steering. In English, the right hand side of a boat is called "starboard", from the Norse word *styra*, meaning "to steer".

Ropes held the sail in place.

Spar

The mast could be lowered during a battle to protect the sail.

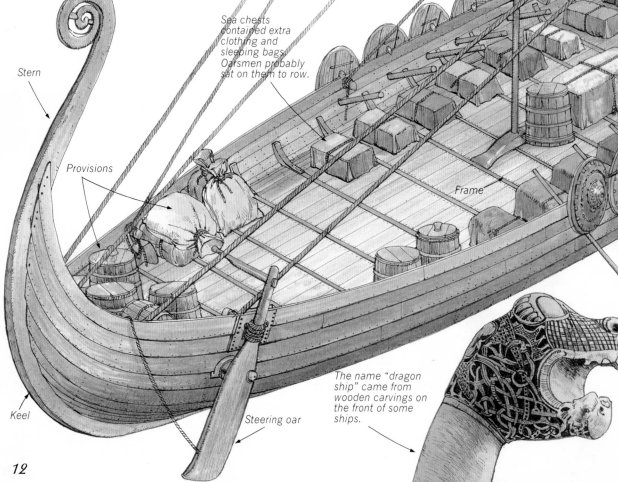

Stern

Sea chests contained extra clothing and sleeping bags. Oarsmen probably sat on them to row.

Provisions

Frame

Keel

Steering oar

The name "dragon ship" came from wooden carvings on the front of some ships.

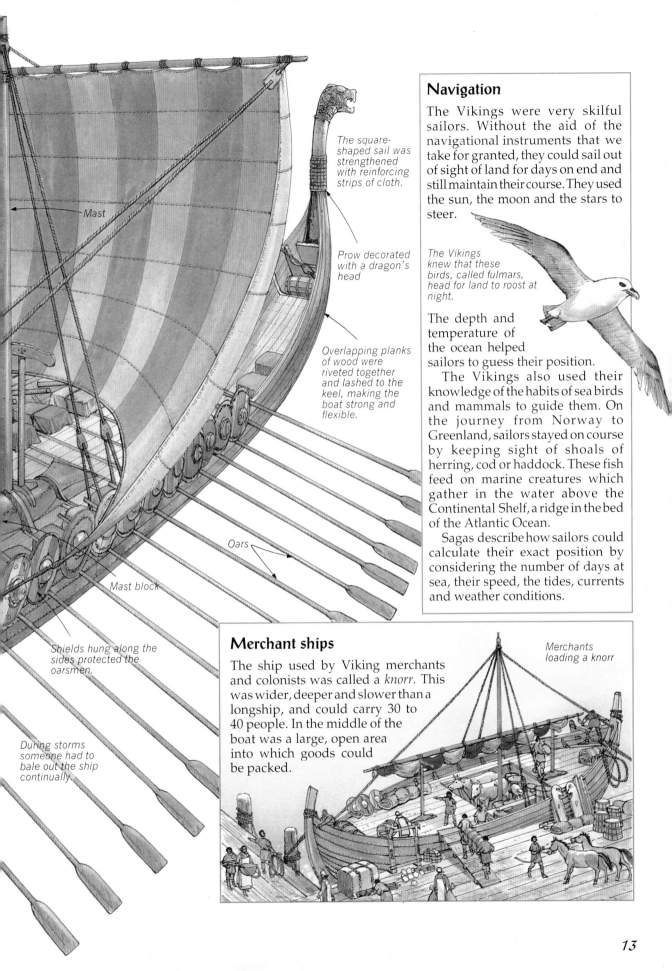

The square-shaped sail was strengthened with reinforcing strips of cloth.

Mast

Prow decorated with a dragon's head

Overlapping planks of wood were riveted together and lashed to the keel, making the boat strong and flexible.

Oars

Mast block

Shields hung along the sides protected the oarsmen.

During storms someone had to bale out the ship continually.

Navigation

The Vikings were very skilful sailors. Without the aid of the navigational instruments that we take for granted, they could sail out of sight of land for days on end and still maintain their course. They used the sun, the moon and the stars to steer.

The Vikings knew that these birds, called fulmars, head for land to roost at night.

The depth and temperature of the ocean helped sailors to guess their position.

The Vikings also used their knowledge of the habits of sea birds and mammals to guide them. On the journey from Norway to Greenland, sailors stayed on course by keeping sight of shoals of herring, cod or haddock. These fish feed on marine creatures which gather in the water above the Continental Shelf, a ridge in the bed of the Atlantic Ocean.

Sagas describe how sailors could calculate their exact position by considering the number of days at sea, their speed, the tides, currents and weather conditions.

Merchant ships

The ship used by Viking merchants and colonists was called a *knorr*. This was wider, deeper and slower than a longship, and could carry 30 to 40 people. In the middle of the boat was a large, open area into which goods could be packed.

Merchants loading a knorr

Viking warriors

The Vikings' reputation as savage fighters made them among the most feared warriors of their time. Even when they were outnumbered, their courage and lightning attacks often gave them an advantage over their enemies. The skill of Viking mercenaries (hired soldiers) was legendary and many rulers were prepared to pay for their service and loyalty.

Local chieftains kept a small band of warriors to act as their bodyguards. Men were trained from boyhood to use weapons, and were expected to defend their country and fight for their chieftain or king when ordered to. Landless men often joined raiding parties, attracted by the promise of treasure and adventure. Even at the end of the Viking Age, the Viking armies which fought campaigns abroad were still made up of volunteers.

A group of Viking warriors launching a surprise attack on a coastal community

Protective clothing

The quality of a warrior's protective clothing depended on his wealth and status. Wealthy men or professional warriors wore a kind of chain mail shirt called a *byrnie*. A *byrnie* was either knee- or hip-length and made of thousands of handmade, inter-locking iron rings. Chain mail was expensive and valuable and was often passed down from father to son. Poorer fighting men had to rely on padded leather jackets to protect them.

Warriors carried large, round wooden shields which were about 1 m (3 ft) in diameter and covered their bodies from chin to knee. The shields

were reinforced with a metal rim. The carrier's hand was protected by a metal cap, called a boss, in the middle of the shield. Some men painted vivid pictures or patterns on their shields.

Most warriors wore helmets made of leather or metal. Some helmets had a rounded top and an eye and nose guard. Others had a conical (slightly pointed) top and a straight nose-piece. In the past, many artists have shown Vikings with helmets decorated with wings or horns. In fact the Vikings did not wear such things.

Some men stayed on board the longship, ready to protect it if necessary.

Spears had an iron point and a wooden shaft.

An axe with a wooden shaft

Padded leather jacket

Some men carried bows and arrows.

A sword carried in a scabbard

Chain mail tunic

A warrior's knife was kept in a leather sheath.

Painted shield with a metal rim

Weapons

Warriors were trained to fight with a wide selection of weapons. They carried two types of spear: light-weight javelins for throwing at the enemy, and heavier, longer spears for thrusting in hand-to-hand combat. Some men had wooden bows and metal-tipped arrows.

A popular weapon was the axe. Viking axes were huge, with 1 m (3 ft) long shafts and rounded blades.

A 10th century axehead decorated with silver wire

Viking swords were held in one hand and their double edges made them perfect for slashing. The blades were about 1 m (3 ft) long and were made of several iron rods twisted together and beaten flat. This made them flexible and hard to shatter.

Many beautiful swords have been found buried with their owners. They were expensive and greatly treasured. Warriors gave their swords names like *Mailbiter*, *Leg-Biter* and *Adder*.

A warrior kept his sword in a holder called a scabbard which was made of wood or leather. The scabbard was either suspended from his belt, or hung across one shoulder using a support called a baldric.

A collection of Viking swords

A sword decorated with gold wire

A sword inscribed with runes* spelling the word "fierce"

Viking armies

During the 9th century, Scandinavian kings and powerful chieftains gathered together forces of several hundred men to join special expeditions to conquer new lands. These armies invaded countries in fleets of hundreds of longships. One such fleet was known as the "Great Army" (see page 33).

In battle, a specially chosen warrior carried a banner, decorated with an emblem such as a serpent or a raven.

The banners Vikings carried into battle may have looked like this.

Some men believed these banners had magical powers which could bring them good luck.

If they were surrounded by their enemies during a battle, Viking warriors formed a bodyguard around their chieftain and used their shields to make a wall. Loyalty to the chieftain was everything. If he was killed, his warriors were expected to fight to the death beside his body.

A blacksmith beating the blade of a sword

Wild warriors

"Berserks" were the most feared group of Viking warriors. Before battle, they made speeches insulting the enemy and boasting of their own excellence. They demonstrated their bravery by fighting without wearing any protective clothing. Some people thought they had magic powers which prevented iron weapons from piercing their skin. One saga describes how some berserks "advanced without mail shirts and were frenzied like mad dogs and wolves, they bit their shields in their fury".

A chess piece in the shape of a berserk chewing his shield.

The professionals

Some men became professional fighters. They formed fellow-ships and lived in communities, obeying strict rules about conduct and duty. Kings hired them as bodyguards, and merchants paid them to protect valuable cargoes.

Sagas tell of a fellowship of warriors, the Jomsvikings, who lived in a fortress called Jomsborg. One evening, while they were drunk, King Harald Blue-Tooth of Denmark made the Jomsvikings swear to defeat his enemy, Earl Hakon of Norway. But they were beaten in battle and imprisoned. The Norwegians began beheading them in turn. One young warrior asked a guard to hold his hair away from his neck to stop it from getting soaked with blood. He jerked his head as the axe fell, and the guard's arm was cut off. The Norwegians were so impressed by his trickery that they offered to release him. He refused to leave without his comrades. So all the Jomsvikings were set free.

Norse women

Viking women enjoyed much more respect and independence than many of their contemporaries in other parts of the world. There are places in Scandinavia named after women, which show that they were allowed to own land and property. Daughters sometimes inherited a share of their parents' wealth. But a woman's status varied according to her position in society. The wife of a wealthy chieftain had more authority and freedom than the wife of a farm worker.

Viking marriages

Parents usually chose wives and husbands for their children. Many matches were made for financial or political reasons, and not for love.

Before a wedding, a bridegroom offered a gift of property of an agreed value to his bride's father. This gift was called the bridesprice. The bride's father provided her with a dowry of goods and money. Her bridesprice and dowry remained the woman's property after she was married.

A Viking marriage ceremony was followed by a large feast to which many guests were invited. One saga describes the marriage of Heidrek and Herborg: "their wedding feast was the greatest the land had ever seen; it lasted for a month".

A housewife's duties

A Viking housewife had many duties cooking, baking and brewing alcoholic drinks for the members of her household. A wealthy woman had slaves to do this work for her.

Spinning and weaving took up a large part of a woman's day. It was up to her to produce all the clothes her family needed. She also made blankets and wove tapestries to decorate the walls of her home.

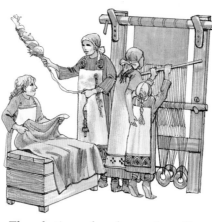

The duties of a farmer's wife included milking cows and sheep, and making butter and cheese. She had to keep chickens and geese and help in the fields at harvest time. It was also her job to arrange household finances and supervise her husband's slaves.

Women looked after their children while they were young and were expected to nurse any members of the household who were sick. In order to do this, they had to know how to mix up remedies using herbs and minerals.

As a sign of her status and responsibility, a housewife always carried the household keys with her. She usually kept them on a chain attached to her tunic brooch. There would have been keys to the door of the house, to her husband's strong box, and to caskets containing jewels, silks or precious spices from the East.

Before Christianity came to Scandinavia, any man who was not a slave was allowed to live with several women if he wanted. He had one proper wife, who was the head of the household and usually came from the same social class as him. The other women were usually household slaves.

Entertaining guests

Vikings prided themselves on their hospitality, and it was considered a disgrace to turn a visitor away from the door. It was a housewife's duty to provide food and shelter for her husband's guests. At a feast, the chieftain's wife served the best food and drink she could find.

During a feast, a chieftain's wife was expected to present gifts to reward her husband's warriors for their loyalty. She might also reward a *skald** for composing a song or poem which flattered her husband's courage in battle and his generosity.

Home alone

If a woman's husband was a warrior or a merchant who spent months raiding or trading abroad, she was responsible for running the farm or business in his absence. She made decisions on her husband's behalf and bargained with visiting merchants.

A noble woman was expected to organize the protection of her home. One saga tells of a woman who chased off attackers herself (see *The story of Freydis*).

Divorce

If a woman wanted to divorce her husband, she simply announced her intentions in front of a group of witnesses. After the separation, she was allowed to keep her dowry and any property she had owned before her marriage. A man could divorce his wife in the same way.

Professional women

Archaeologists have found evidence which shows that a few Viking women had unusual professions. Some written sources mention female skalds and a female carver of *runes**. One woman's grave has been found containing scales, weights and measures, which suggest she was a merchant or worked in a market.

Some women took a leading part in the religious ceremonies and rituals that were held to worship the Norse gods. Certain women were thought to be prophetesses, who were able to foretell the future and give people advice in their daily lives.

The story of Freydis

One saga tells the story of a famous Viking woman, Freydis, daughter of Eric the Red. She was a member of an expedition to North America. One morning a party of native American Indians attacked the settlement. Freydis frightened them off by charging at them, beating her chest with a sword.

Later, when a quarrel broke out in the camp between Freydis and two brothers, she persuaded her husband to kill the brothers and their men. She took an axe and killed their wives herself.

Children

In Viking times, women often died in childbirth and many children died young. Babies were sometimes left outside to die if they were badly handicapped, or if their parents were too poor to raise them.

Children had to learn the skills they would need as adults. Boys were taught to hunt and handle weapons. They learned farming or a craft. Some men took their sons on trading voyages to teach them how to sail. Girls learned to cook, make cloth and care for babies.

Viking towns

Most settlements in Viking times were small farming communities which developed in areas of fertile land. There were a few large towns which grew into important trading posts. The most famous of these were Hedeby in Denmark and Birka in Sweden. Archaeologists have also excavated Viking towns at York in England and Dublin in Ireland.

Viking towns were crowded and dirty, with the smoke from many household fires polluting the air. Craftsmen were attracted to towns for protection and to be near their customers. Merchants of many nationalities came to buy Viking goods such as slaves, furs, walrus ivory and falcons. They also bought items that Viking merchants had brought back from the East such as silks, spices and wine.

This is a reconstruction of a Viking trading town and its port.

Merchant ships full of valuable cargo

A barrier made of wood called a palisade to shelter ships and prevent attack

Warehouses

Barrels of wine

Workshops

A sh... mak...

A merchant selling furs from Russia

A fish seller

Soapstone bowls

Glass brought from the East

Tannery*

A chieftain and his son in town to buy a ship for raiding

A house made of wattle and daub (see opposite page)

A smith at his forge

A merchant selling swords

An Arab trader selling silk

People buying wine in exchange for slaves

Money and coins

At the beginning of the Viking Age, people bartered one kind of goods for another. They also paid for things with carefully weighed out quantities of silver. The silver was either jewellery or foreign coins which traders brought back from abroad.

By the 10th century, coins were widely used throughout Scandinavia. A craftsman called a "moneyer" stamped them out from a strip of silver using a die.

A moneyer at work

A selection of Viking coins

Enclosure for sheep and goats

A roof being thatched

House made of split tree trunks

Potter

Geese

Boundary fence between houses

Animal sacrificed to the gods

Toilet

Town houses

Town houses were small, with up to three rooms. Some were built of wooden planks; others were made of wattle and daub (a framework made of twigs woven together and covered in a mixture of straw and mud). Most houses had thatched roofs, which meant there was always a risk of fires.

Loom

Wooden walkways

Viking society and government

In early Viking times, Scandinavia was divided into several kingdoms. But the kings were not very powerful, because most communities were loyal to their local chieftain. A king had to conduct religious rituals and lead his subjects into battle. He was expected to keep a force of fighting men and ships to protect his people and their property from attack.

A Viking king

When a king died, his oldest son did not automatically succeed him. A new king would be chosen from the members of the reigning royal family. A candidate's age, health, reputation and popularity were all taken into consideration.

Apart from royalty, there were three main groups in Viking society: *jarls*, *karls* and *thralls*.

Jarls

Jarls were the wealthiest, most powerful people. They were the Viking chieftains, aristocracy and often owned and ruled large areas of land. A jarl usually had a small band of household warriors to fight for him when needed. If he decided to go *a-Viking* (see page 5), many men from his community would also join the expedition.

A wealthy jarl and his family

Karls

The largest group in Viking society were the karls, who were free men and women. Many karls owned their own farmsteads; others rented land from rich landowners. In Viking times, a man's land was usually inherited by his eldest son. Younger sons had to make their own forutnes, so they joined raiding parties to find riches abroad or became professional warriors or mechants. Others became hunters, fishermen or craftsmen. The poorest landless karls were servants or farm workers.

A blacksmith and a woman making combs from antlers

Thralls

Viking slaves were called thralls. They did not have any rights and were bought and sold like any other piece of property.

Many slaves were captured in raids or wars. Some were karls who had lost their freedom after going bankrupt or committing a crime. The children of thralls had the same status as their parents.

Most slaves worked as household servants or farm workers. A few slaves were craftsmen who earned a wage. Those who worked hard, and saved money could buy freedom for their families and themselves.

Family feuds

Family ties and loyalties were very important to the Vikings. People were prepared to fight to the death to defend the honour of their families. An insult or injury done to one person might lead the whole family to seek revenge. A violent and bloody feud between two families could last for years.

Viking honour

A Viking's honour and good name was his or her most highly prized possession. A good reputation depended on a variety of things. A warrior's worth was judged by his courage, his fighting skills, how far afield his adventures had taken him, and how successful and lucrative his expeditions were.

Merchants, craftsmen and farmers were respected most for intelligence and honesty, their ability to do good deeds and to keep their word once it was given.

All freemen and women were expected to be loyal to their friends, their followers and their chieftain.

Viking government

The Vikings held local open-air meetings, called *Things*, where they discussed any problems that affected local people, settled disputes and punished criminals. *Things* were held every two or three years. All freemen were allowed to attend the meetings and voice their own opinions on any issue.

In early Viking times, decisions on cases brought before a *Thing* were made by all those present. Later, judges were chosen by the people or by the king.

In Iceland, a national *Thing*, called an *Althing*, was held every year. At this meeting laws were passed which affected everyone on the island. The *Althing* was held during the summer, when people found it easiest to travel long distances overland.

Trials and punishments

Anyone suspected of a crime stood trial. If the evidence against them was inconclusive, other methods were used to decide their guilt or innocence. For example, people could be tried by ordeal. Women had to pick stones out of boiling water and men had to carry red hot iron a few paces. If they dropped the stones or the iron, they were considered guilty. Those who managed their tasks had their wounds bound. They were examined after a week. If the wounds were healing well, the person was declared innocent. Some men chose to undergo trial by combat to settle a dispute. They fought until one man was killed or surrendered.

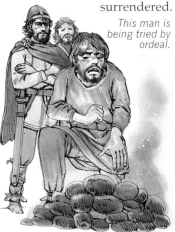

This man is being tried by ordeal.

A criminal's punishment was decided by the *Thing*. He could be fined, reduced to slavery or even outlawed. An outlawed man had to flee, because he was outside the protection of the law and anyone could kill him.

Vikings believed that everyone was worth a certain sum of money, called their *wergeld*. A warrior's *wergeld* was more than a poor fisherman's. A murderer had to pay a *wergeld* to his victim's parents.

The Icelandic **Althing** was held at a place called Thingvellir meaning "Thing plain".

A tent like this was found on the Oseberg burial ship.

Merchants selling their wares

Horses were used for riding or carrying packs.

Viking wagons had round-bottomed bodies fastened to the undercarriage with ropes.

Judge

This man has been found guilty of robbery and will be outlawed.

Camp fire

Death and burial in Viking times

The Vikings believed in a life after death. They thought that anything buried with a dead person would accompany him or her to the next life. So people were buried with their possessions. Many graves have been found containing hoards of treasure, tools, food and drink and weapons. Some rich people even had their slaves buried with them to serve them in the next life.

Graves and grave goods

The size of a Viking grave, the quality of its grave goods, and the type of monument built to mark its position, reflected the wealth and status of its occupant.

The poor were buried in holes in the ground. The body was placed in a hollowed-out tree trunk or in a simple wooden box. A low mound of earth was piled on top of the grave site.

This woman was dressed in her best clothes and buried with a barrel of milk, a comb and some bobbins for spinning.

Wealthy Vikings could afford more lavish burials. Their graves were large and lined with wood. Merchants were buried with their weighing scales and their silver. Some people had horses or dogs buried with them.

A slave girl was killed and buried with her master. Two of the chieftain's best horses have also been placed in the grave.

Royal burials

The most spectacular burials took place when a royal or powerful Viking died. The body and grave goods were put in a ship which was then buried or burned. The Vikings believed that the ship with its occupant sailed off to Asgard, the land of the Norse gods.

In 921, an Arab diplomat called Ibn Fadlan was journeying in Russia. He met a band of Viking warrior merchants, known as the Rus (see pages 40 and 41). Fadlan witnessed a chieftain's body being cremated in a ship and wrote an account of what he had seen.

The dead chieftain was laid in a tent on the deck of a longship. Around him, his family and friends packed many beautiful treasures and other possessions. A slave girl, who had volunteered to accompany her master into the next life, was given a pain-killing drink. Then an old woman, known as the "Angel of Death", strangled the girl whose body was placed on the ship with the chieftain. The ship and its contents were set on fire. Later, a mound of earth was piled over the ashes.

This is a reconstruction of the kind of ship-cremation Ibn Fadlan watched.

The chieftain's body is inside this tent on deck.

Memorial stones

Some people set up stones in memory of their dead relatives, particularly Vikings who had died abroad and whose bodies had not been brought home. Memorial stones had inscriptions or pictures on them.

Memorial stones

Some people who could not afford a ship burial had graves outlined with stones in the shape of a boat.

A casket of silver and jewels and two of the chieftain's horses are on board.

Warriors set fire to the boat.

Slave girl

Burial ships

In 1880, a Viking burial ship was uncovered in Gokstad, Norway. It had been built in about 850 and perhaps 50 years later it was hauled ashore for a royal funeral. The blue clay around the ship had kept it almost perfectly preserved. Inside a small wooden chamber on deck was the body of a king. His huge cargo of burial goods included six dogs, 12 horses and a peacock.

A Viking ship built 50 years earlier than the Gokstad ship was excavated at Oseberg, Norway, in 1903. The bodies of a queen and her maid were found on board. Packed into the hold of the ship was a collection of beautifully decorated wooden furniture, including four sledges, three beds and many kitchen utensils.

The prow of the Gokstad burial ship

The Oseberg ship's beautifully carved stern after restoration

Archaeologists with the Oseberg ship while it was being excavated

A wooden sledge and a pair of skis for journeys in the Next World

The "Angel of Death"

The Next World

The Vikings told many stories about the Next World. They believed that, after death, those people who had led a good and honest life were taken to Asgard, where they lived in the hall of the god or goddess they worshipped.

The souls of less worthy people were taken to the land of the dead, which was ruled by the goddess Hel. She was a very beautiful woman, but from the waist downward she was a hideous skeleton. Her hall was called Eljundir and its entrance was guarded by a ferocious dog who ensured those who entered could never escape.

The Vikings believed that some souls, known as "dead walkers", came back to haunt the living. They could be vicious and possessed supernatural strength.

The goddess Hel

The death of a warrior

The greatest honour for a Viking warrior was to die fighting. According to legend, the Viking god Odin had a group of female attendants, called Valkyries, who flew over battlefields and snatched up the souls of brave warriors who lay dead. They took these souls to Valhalla, Odin's hall, which had rafters made of spears and walls made of shields.

The warriors who lived in Valhalla perfected their fighting skills all day and feasted all night. Some legends say that they were busily preparing their weapons and themselves to help the Norse gods fight the forces of evil at Ragnarok (see page 51).

(see page 51)

This picture of Valhalla is from a 13th century Icelandic manuscript.

Valhalla is said to have had hundreds of doors.

Odin is shown standing in front of the hall.

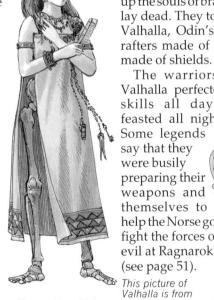

Norse gods and goddesses

The Vikings worshipped many different gods and goddesses who affected every aspect of their lives and the world they lived in. They believed the deities controlled what happened to people after they died.

The Norse universe

The Norse universe had three levels. On the highest level was a heavenly place called Asgard, where the gods lived in magnificent halls, with their servants and followers.

On the middle level was the world were humans lived, called Midgard. Asgard and Midgard were connected by a flaming rainbow bridge called Bifrost. Surrounding Midgard was an ocean inhabited by a serpent called Jormungand.

The lowest level contained the land of the dead, called Niflheim, an icy place of eternal darkness, and Muspellheim, the land of fire.

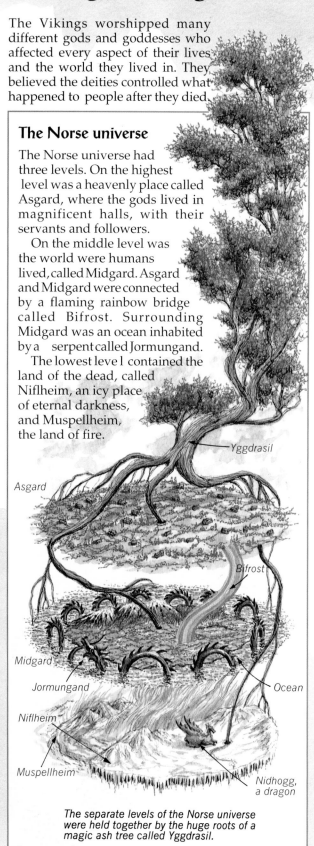

The separate levels of the Norse universe were held together by the huge roots of a magic ash tree called Yggdrasil.

Labels on illustration: Yggdrasil, Asgard, Bifrost, Midgard, Jormungand, Ocean, Niflheim, Muspellheim, Nidhogg, a dragon

Norse gods and goddesses

There were two main types of Norse gods and goddesses: the Vanir and the Aesir. The Vanir were fertility deities, who made crops grow and were worshipped by farmers. Fighting men worshipped the Aesir, who were warrior gods. Some of the most important Viking deities are described below.

Frey

Odin and Frigg

Odin was the king of the gods and ruler of all things. He was feared by humans and gods alike. As the god of battle, he is said to have caused wars on earth by throwing down his magic spear. As the god of poetry, he inspired storytellers and Viking poets (called skalds).

Odin had only one eye, because he had sacrificed the other one to gain knowledge and understanding. You can read this legend on page 50. He rode a magnificent eight-legged horse called Sleipnir. On his shoulders perched two ravens called Thought and Memory. Every day these birds flew around the world and returned to tell Odin what they had seen.

Odin's wife was the goddess Frigg, renowned for her kindness and beauty. She looked after the health and well-being of all human beings, especially children. She had a very strong character and could even outwit Odin if she wished.

Frigg

Thor

Thor was the son of Odin and the Earth. He was well known for his love of huge feasts, excessive drinking and ferocious fighting. His fiery temper was said to match his flame red hair and beard.

As the god of law and order, he controlled his enemies with his incredible strength and his magic hammer called Mjollnir. Thor raced through the skies in a chariot drawn by two giant goats. People thought that the sound of thunder was the clatter of the chariot's wheels.

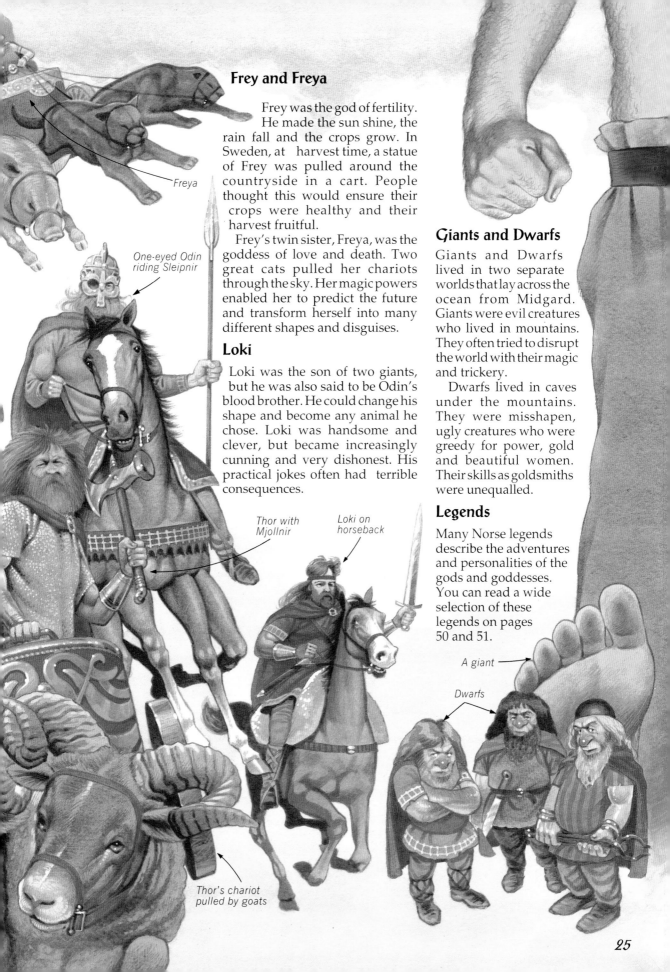

Frey and Freya

Frey was the god of fertility. He made the sun shine, the rain fall and the crops grow. In Sweden, at harvest time, a statue of Frey was pulled around the countryside in a cart. People thought this would ensure their crops were healthy and their harvest fruitful.

Frey's twin sister, Freya, was the goddess of love and death. Two great cats pulled her chariots through the sky. Her magic powers enabled her to predict the future and transform herself into many different shapes and disguises.

Loki

Loki was the son of two giants, but he was also said to be Odin's blood brother. He could change his shape and become any animal he chose. Loki was handsome and clever, but became increasingly cunning and very dishonest. His practical jokes often had terrible consequences.

Giants and Dwarfs

Giants and Dwarfs lived in two separate worlds that lay across the ocean from Midgard. Giants were evil creatures who lived in mountains. They often tried to disrupt the world with their magic and trickery.

Dwarfs lived in caves under the mountains. They were misshapen, ugly creatures who were greedy for power, gold and beautiful women. Their skills as goldsmiths were unequalled.

Legends

Many Norse legends describe the adventures and personalities of the gods and goddesses. You can read a wide selection of these legends on pages 50 and 51.

Freya

One-eyed Odin riding Sleipnir

Thor with Mjollnir

Loki on horseback

A giant

Dwarfs

Thor's chariot pulled by goats

Worshipping the Norse gods

Little is known about how and where the Vikings worshipped their gods and goddesses. The only surviving accounts of their rituals are rather unreliable because they were written either by Arab visitors, who were Muslims and were probably hostile toward the Norse religion, or by Christian monks and priests, who were writing centuries after the Vikings' religion had died out.

Temples and holy places

Vikings usually conducted their religious ceremonies in the open air, among groves of trees, on hillsides or beside springs. These were considered holy places.

The Vikings also built temples to worship in. One written account describes a richly decorated building, with elaborately carved pillars, golden ornaments and statues of Norse deities. Another document describes a temple which contained a life-sized statue of Thor sitting in a chariot pulled by rams. But little remains of these religious sites, because they were destroyed when Christianity spread through Scandinavia.

Rituals and ceremonies

Religious rituals were conducted by local leaders, such as chieftains or rich farmers. They performed sacrifices to the gods on behalf of the people in their communities, and offered weapons and jewels, by throwing them into bogs or rivers.

At Uppsala in Sweden and Lejre in Denmark, a huge festival was held every ninth year. Adam, a Christian monk from Bremen, Germany, wrote an account of what took place at the Uppsala festival which lasted nine days and nights. Every day a man and a variety of male animals were sacrificed and their bodies hung on trees in a grove near the temple. At Lejre, 99 men and 99 horses, dogs and cocks were sacrificed and hung in a sacred grove.

Experts think that this section of a 9th century tapestry shows a religious procession.

This picture shows a procession of Viking men and women attending a religious ceremony.

Worship at home

Vikings prayed to the gods for help in their everyday lives, reciting spells and asked for protection against evil spirits. They believed witches used clippings from a victim's hair or nails to gain control of them. Many people wore protective charms, called amulets, to bring them good fortune.

Amulets shaped like Thor's hammer

Al-Tartushi, an Arab merchant, visited Hedeby, Denmark, in the 10th century. He described how a man who had sacrificed an ox, goat or pig would display the animal on a wooden scaffold beside his house, to show onlookers that he had paid tribute to the gods.

Two men and a bull have been sacrificed.

Amulets

A procession of worshippers

Food has been brought in buckets to be offered to the gods.

Statues of Viking gods

This chieftain is performing the ceremony at an altar made of a large stone.

Feasts

Feasts were an important part of Viking life. They were held to celebrate religious festivals, weddings and funerals. The family and friends of a chieftain or rich farmer dressed in their finest clothes and gathered in his hall. Many stories describe feasts as boisterous occasions which could last as long as two weeks.

A reconstruction of a Viking feast

The chieftain

Men hung up their weapons as a sign of good will.

Guests were entertained by storytellers and by poets called skalds, who recited poems.

Hosts displayed their wealth by serving rich meals and much ale.

Acrobats and jugglers

Wine, a great luxury, was shipped from France.

Foretelling the future

The Vikings believed in the art of prophecy, and their goddess Freya (see page 25) was thought to have prophetic powers. Some women, who were followers of Freya, claimed to be able to predict the future and interpret dreams. They journeyed around the countryside in groups, staying at the halls of local leaders.

During a religious ceremony, the chief prophetess sat on a platform or a special chair. Her companions chanted sacred songs and spells, and she fell into a trance. People believed that her soul left her body and soared over the earth, giving her great insight and wisdom. Afterwards, she told people about future events and how to find health and happiness.

Sagas

The Vikings told long exciting tales of famous battles and adventures. These detailed stories are called sagas and are a rich source of information about the Vikings' way of life, culture and ideals. The first sagas to be written down were recorded by Christian monks in Iceland during the 12th century.

Runes

The Viking system of writing was made up of marks or letters called runes. The angular shape of runes made them easy to carve or scratch into stones, bones or wood.

The Viking alphabet was known as *futhark*, after the sounds of the first six runes. It contained 16 runes in total, which was not enough for every sound in the language. This made spelling words very difficult.

The runes most commonly used during Viking times are shown below, with their equivalent sounds in the modern alphabet. (You can read a legend about how the god Odin brought back the runes from the Land of the Dead on page 50.)

The runic alphabet

ᚠᚢᚦᚨᚱᚲ
f u th a r k

ᚺᚾᛁᚨᛋ ᛏᛒᛘᛚᛦ
h n i a s t b m l r

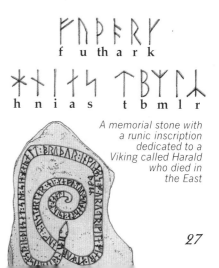

A memorial stone with a runic inscription dedicated to a Viking called Harald who died in the East

Christianity during the Viking Age

The Christian church was first established in Palestine by the followers of Jesus of Nazareth (c.5 B.C.-A.D.29). In the centuries after his death, Christianity spread rapidly through the Roman Empire. But it was almost wiped out in some places during the 4th and the 5th centuries, when migrating tribes conquered Roman lands (see page 4).

Surviving Christians began to go out and tell people about their beliefs. Missionaries sent by the Pope (the head of the Catholic church) were very successful in their attempts to convert the people in the new kingdoms of western Europe.

During the 9th and 10th centuries, missionaries from Rome and from Constantinople began working among the people of central and eastern Europe. Their preaching led to mass conversions among the Magyars (who settled in Hungary) and the Slavs (from eastern Europe and Russia).

A bishop's staff stolen from Ireland by Vikings

Converting the Vikings

Throughout most of the Viking Age, the people of Scandinavia worshipped their own gods and goddesses. But by the end of the period these had been replaced by Christianity. The first Vikings to come into contact with Christians were probably raiders and traders, who were impressed by the ceremonies and churches in western Europe.

Scandinavians who settled in countries which had already adopted the Christian faith (such as England, Ireland and France) quickly converted to the new religion. Viking merchants also found it useful to become Christians, as it made them more acceptable to their customers.

Christianity in Scandinavia

The conversion of Scandinavia to Christianity took almost two centuries. The first Christians to go there were probably slaves captured on raids, or European merchants who visited towns such as Birka and Hedeby.

Later missionaries were sent to all the Scandinavian countries. They were eager to convert the Vikings. Their reason was not only to preach the teachings of Christ to all people, they also saw it as a way of stopping the raids which were terrorizing people all over Europe. Monasteries and churches were among the Vikings' main targets.

Missionaries in Denmark

The first missionaries arrived in Denmark in the 8th century. At first their success was limited. Most were simply ignored, others ended up as slaves and the unluckiest were killed.

In c.965, Harald Blue-Tooth, the King of Denmark, became a Christian. Only a few of his subjects

Crucifixes found in Scandinavia

followed his example whole-heartedly, but he claimed in a runic inscription on the Jelling Stone (shown here) to have "made the Danes Christians".

Harald Blue-Tooth's rune-stone, known as the Jelling Stone, shows a picture of Jesus Christ.

During the reign of Harald's grandson, Cnut, who was King of Denmark and England, English missionaries worked steadily at converting the Danes. Eventually, the Danish people fully accepted Christianity and, in 1104, a Danish man was made an archbishop, one of the highest ranking clergymen in the Catholic church.

The conversion of Norway

The Norwegians were persuaded to adopt the Christian faith by two of their kings, Olaf Tryggvason and Olaf Haraldsson. Both kings used threats and violence to force some of their subjects to be baptized.

A missionary teaching Magyars about the life of Jesus of Nazareth.

Olaf Haraldsson was made the first patron saint of Scandinavia. After his death, people claimed to see miracles at the site of his grave.

Christianity in the colonies

Olaf Tryggvason used great force to persuade the settlers in Iceland to become Christians. For example, he threatened to kill any Icelanders living in or visiting Norway unless the islanders converted. They finally agreed to Christianity becoming the official religion after a long debate at the *Althing*. But for years after this, many people on the island secretly worshipped Norse gods.

One legend describes how Leif Ericsson visited Norway and was converted to Christianity by Olaf Tryggvason. Leif returned home to Greenland and encouraged the islanders to follow his example.

Sweden finally succumbs

Sweden was the last country in Scandinavia to adopt Christianity. Missionaries were sent by the Catholic church in Germany to work amongst the Swedes. King Olof Skötkonung of Sweden was baptized in 1008, and Christianity became the country's official religion. But many Swedes continued to worship the Norse gods, keeping the old religion alive for almost a century. Olof caused a public uprising when he ordered his men to cut down the sacred groves where the Vikings worshipped. Statues of the Norse gods were taken down and dragged through the streets.

Destroying the groves

Christianity and the end of the Viking Age

For many years the old religion and the new existed side by side. Some people simply added the Christian God to the collection of Norse gods they already worshipped.

This smith's cast produced an amulet in the shape of Thor's hammer and two crosses.

The churches were made of wood with intricate carvings.

Crosses and dragons' heads decorate the roofs of the church.

These dragons' heads are similar to those used on Viking ships.

But when Scandinavia finally accepted Christianity, the Viking way of life was forced to change dramatically. Viking customs, such as sacrificing human beings, killing weak children and burying grave goods with people, were forbidden in a Christian society.

Gradually Christian churches, like this one, were built throughout Scandinavia.

A wooden church in Borgund, Norway, built c.1150

The age of kings

Before the Viking Age, there were several kingdoms in Scandinavia, ruled by kings or chieftains. Each region had its own laws and customs. There was no centralized royal power because people were loyal to local leaders.

During the time of the Vikings, Norway, Sweden and Denmark developed into separate countries, each united under a single monarch. As the importance

A chieftain's helmet from pre-Viking times

of trade, towns and foreign relations grew, people began to see the advantages of the stability and order that a strong monarch could give. Some of the events in the reigns of the early kings of Scandinavia are described below.

Denmark

Denmark was ruled by one king as early as the 9th century, but little is known about its kings until Harald Blue-Tooth came to power in 950. He enjoyed a long and prosperous reign, and his kingdom included the southern tip of Norway (see the map on page 5).

During his reign, Harald is thought to have built royal fortresses like the one shown below. He used them to reinforce his personal and military power following his defeat by the German emperor in 974 at Danevirke on his southern border.

Sweyn Forkbeard, Harald's son, grew tired of waiting to inherit the throne. In 987, he overthrew his father and seized the crown. Harald died soon afterward. Sweyn was a ruthless military leader. He maintained Danish control over Norway and conquered England in 1013. He died a year later.

Royal fortresses in Denmark

Archaeologists have found the remains of four royal fortresses which they believe were built by King Harald Blue-Tooth. The fortresses were used as bases from which the surrounding country-side was ruled. Circular in shape, they had four entrances, and the barracks in which the warriors lived formed four rectangles.

A cut-away picture of one of the barrack houses

This picture shows a reconstruction of the royal fortress at Trelleborg, West Zealand in Denmark.

A plan of the fortress showing its symmetrical shape

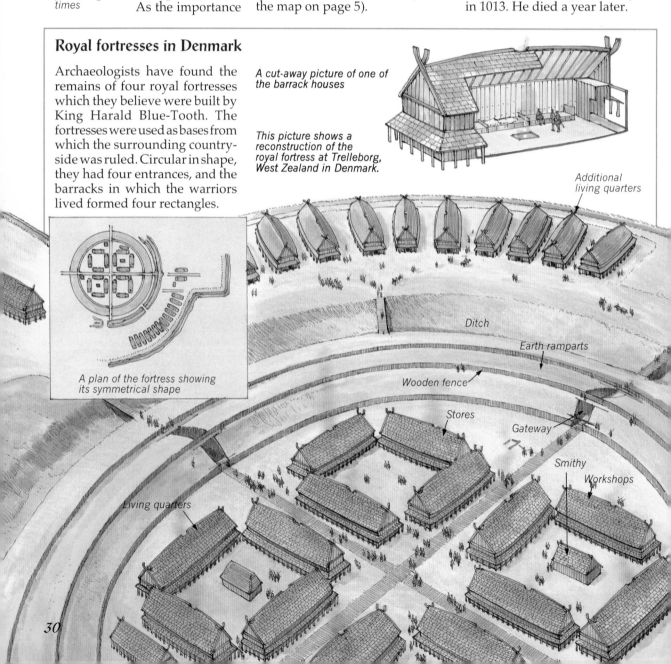

Additional living quarters

Ditch

Earth ramparts

Wooden fence

Stores

Gateway

Smithy

Workshops

Living quarters

30

Cnut the Great

Sweyn's son Cnut inherited the Danish empire from his father in 1014. He was the most powerful king to rule during the Viking Age. By seizing part of Sweden, he enlarged the area under his control. But when he died in 1035 his empire soon disintegrated. Stability returned to Denmark only when Sweyn Estridsson, Cnut's nephew, came to power in 1047.

King Cnut

Norway

Norway was united under a single king in about 880, when Harald Finehair became King of Norway. He was a popular king, celebrated in poems and sagas.

Harald's son, Eric Bloodaxe, inherited the throne in c.930. Eric was harsh and cruel, and he was soon overthrown and the throne was given instead to his brother Hakon. But Hakon was killed in 960, in a battle waged by the sons of Eric Bloodaxe, led by one of the sons, Harald Grey-cloak.

Harald Grey-cloak ruled for ten years before he was deposed by an alliance between Harald Blue-Tooth and Jarl Hakon of Hladir. Jarl Hakon was a powerful Norwegian chieftain who was seeking revenge for the death of his father, at the hands of Harald Grey-cloak. The victors divided Norway between them, with King Harald acting as overall ruler.

Olaf Tryggvason

In 995, Harald Finehair's grandson Olaf Tryggvason returned to Norway after raiding abroad. He drove out Jarl Hakon and seized the throne.

Olaf Tryggvason ruled for five years, until he was deposed by Sweyn Forkbeard, King Olof of Sweden and Jarl Hakon's son Eric.

The battle which followed was fought at sea in longships. When Olaf Tryggvason realized his men were heavily outnumbered and facing imminent defeat, he leapt overboard, preferring to drown, rather than be captured and humiliated by the enemy. Some stories claim he survived and went on to become a monk in Syria.

Olaf Tryggvason leaping overboard during the battle

Olaf Haraldsson

After the battle, Norway was shared between the victors. But in 1015 the throne was seized by Olaf Haraldsson (another of Harald Finehair's descendants). He concentrated on forcing his subjects to become Christians and strengthening his hold on the Orkney and Shetland Islands. He also reformed his country's laws.

In 1028, Olaf and the King of Sweden waged war on Cnut of Denmark. They were defeated by Cnut's army and Olaf was exiled to Russia. He returned to attempt to regain his throne in 1030, but was killed at the Battle of Stiklestad.

An illustration of Olaf Haraldsson being killed at the Battle of Stiklestad

Harald Hardrada

In 1035, Olaf Haraldsson's son Magnus the Good returned from exile in Russia. The people of Norway chose him as king in preference to the Danish king, Cnut. When Magnus died in 1047 without an heir, his uncle, Harald Hardrada (meaning "the ruthless"), became King of Norway.

At the age of fifteen, Harald was wounded at the Battle of Stiklestad in 1030. He escaped to Kiev, where he served in the army of King Yaroslav before joining the Varangian Guard in Constantinople (see page 43).

(see page 43).

Harald was a powerful king, but his reign was plagued by conflict within Norway and a war against Sweyn Forkbeard of Denmark. He was eventually forced to give up the Danish throne, although the Norwegian throne remained in his family for many generations.

Harald in the uniform of a Varangian

Sweden

At the beginning of the Viking Age, Sweden was divided between two peoples called the Svear and the Gautes. By the 8th century, the Svear were the more dominant. According to sagas and legends, the first powerful Swedish king was called Eric the Victorious. He ruled Sweden at the end of the 10th century.

Eric's son Olof Skötkonung became ruler in 995 and converted to Christianity in 1008. He tried to make it the national religion. But most of his subjects still worshipped the Norse gods and his reign was plagued by uprisings. The people rebelled furiously when Olof's men destroyed the temple at Uppsala.

The raiding begins

Norwegian and Danish raiders first appeared off English shores in the early 790s. The inhabitants of England, the Anglo-Saxons, were a Christian people, farmers, scholars and craftsmen. To the men from the North, their land was a perfect target for raiding and colonizing.

This Anglo-Saxon monk is decorating a manuscript with gold leaf.

Raiders arrive in England

In 793, a band of warriors attacked St. Cuthbert's church on the island of Lindisfarne on the northeast coast. They slaughtered many monks, destroyed the church and looted its treasures. Similar asssults on Iona and Jarrow soon followed.

Most Viking raids took place in summer, when the weather was good for sailing. The raiders usually came under the cover of night or fog. They sailed or rowed their longships far inland, up rivers and estuaries. Then the ships were beached and the warriors disembarked and began terrorizing coastal communities, looting, raping and killing as they went.

Some captives were taken. The important people were held for ransom; the rest were usually taken back to Scandinavia to be sold as slaves. Raids lasted only a few days and so the warriors were often back at sea before a rescue party could be gathered together.

Raids on England became very frequent, but from 851, the nature of the Viking attacks changed. Raiding parties began staying in England over winter and built camps, instead of sailing home to Scandinavia.

A monastery under attack

The Vikings have set fire to the monastery and the village.

Slaves are led off to the Vikings' longships.

Monastery

Warriors kill the fleeing monks and steal the monastery's treasures.

Viking warriors pound the gate with a battering ram.

Anglo-Saxons fight back

Some Anglo-Saxon leaders successfully resisted the Vikings. One King of Northumbria captured a Viking leader called Ragnar Lodbrok, known as "Hairy Breeches". According to legend, Lodbrok was thrown into a pit full of poisonous snakes, where he died painfully.

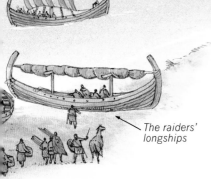

The raiders' longships

The Great Army

In 865, a huge Danish fleet set out to conquer England. The force became known as the "Great Army". It was led by three sons of Ragnar Lodbrok, who came to avenge their father's death.

The Great Army landed and began slaughtering the people of East Anglia. The following year, they captured York. By 869, they had seized land all over Northumbria, East Anglia and Mercia. Ragnar's sons caught their father's killer, the King of Northumbria, and tortured him to death.

Alfred the Great

In 870, part of the Great Army, led by a Dane called Guthrum, marched on Wessex, the most powerful kingdom in England. But Alfred, King of Wessex (later known as "the Great"), gathered an army to resist them.

This jewel may have belonged to Alfred. The inscription says "Alfred ordered me to be made".

Alfred suffered many setbacks. After one vicious surprise attack by the Vikings, he and his household warriors just managed to escape capture by hiding in the Somerset marshes.

Alfred reorganized his army and started building fortified towns and a navy of his own. He finally defeated the Danes at the Battle of Edington in 878.

The Danelaw

After his victory, Alfred was able to force the Danes to accept him as their overlord. He also forced them to become Christians. According to the terms of a treaty signed by Alfred and Guthrum, the Vikings were allowed to occupy an area east of a line running from Chester to London. Within this area, which is known as the Danelaw, Danes were allowed to live in accordance with their own customs and laws.

But the peace brought by the creation of the Danelaw was short-lived. Alfred's descendants wanted the Scandinavians off English soil altogether. In 926, Alfred's grandson, Athelstan, defeated the Danes at the Battle of Brunanburgh, he seized the Danelaw and became the first King of all England.

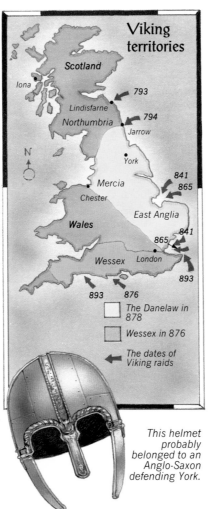

Viking territories

Scotland

Iona

793

Lindisfarne
Northumbria

794

Jarrow

N

York

841
865

Mercia

Chester

East Anglia

841

Wales

865

Wessex   London

893

893   876

☐ The Danelaw in 878

☐ Wessex in 876

← The dates of Viking raids

This helmet probably belonged to an Anglo-Saxon defending York.

The Danegeld

Anglo-Saxon kings ruled England until the reign of Ethelred (978-1016), when there was a new wave of Viking raiding. Ethelred, a weak leader, gave the Danes a large amount of silver to go away. This money was known as Danegeld and was raised by taxes. The Danes took the silver, but soon returned for more. Ethelred grew desperate and ordered the killing of all Danes living on English soil. Many of them were murdered and this event is known as the Massacre of St. Brice's Day.

Silver coins used to pay Danegeld

King Sweyn Forkbeard

Angered by the murder of so many of his countrymen, King Sweyn Forkbeard of Denmark invaded England in 1013. In an attempt to stop the destruction Sweyn's army was causing, the Anglo-Saxons offered him the English throne. But Sweyn ruled England for only a year before he died.

King Cnut

Sweyn's son, King Cnut of Denmark, became the King of England in 1016. He married Ethelred's widow, and to show his willingness to act like an Anglo-Saxon king, he sent home part of the Danish fleet. He kept a bodyguard of only two thousand men and even used English advisers to help him rule wisely.

When Cnut died, his sons fought each other for the throne, but it was given to, Ethelred's son Edward.

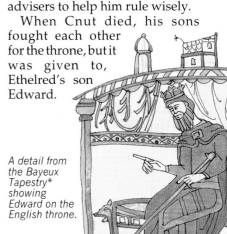

A detail from the Bayeux Tapestry showing Edward on the English throne.*

Exploring the northern seas

In the late 8th century, Norwegian raiding parties sailed west, across the North Sea, looking for new, poorly defended land to raid and plunder. First they reached the Shetland Islands, which were only a 24 hour voyage from Norway with a good wind. From there they sailed to other islands, including the Orkneys, the Faroes and the Hebrides. Some raiding parties continued on to the mainland of Scotland, while others journeyed south to Wales and Ireland.

Map: Scotland, Wales and Ireland — showing Shetland Islands, Orkney Islands, Hebrides, Scotland, Iona, ATLANTIC OCEAN, NORTH SEA, Ireland, Armagh, Dublin, Man, Limerick, Wexford, Waterford, Cork, Wales. Areas of Viking settlement. Long-phorts.

Islands in the Atlantic

Some of the islands in the Atlantic had originally been discovered and settled by Irish monks in the 6th century. But many of these monks fled when the Vikings arrived.

The Vikings used the islands as bases from which they raided Ireland and Scotland. Eventually some of the Norwegians settled peacefully in the places they had plundered. They found farming the conditions very similar to those in Scandinavia and they prospered.

The Faroes became a useful stopping-off point for the Viking explorers who sailed farther west to Iceland, Greenland and even as far as North America.

These Vikings on the Faroes are stripping blubber from a whale.

Scotland

Raiding parties sailed toward Scotland, plundering the Islands of Skye and Iona on their way. The monastery on Iona was so savagely attacked in 795, 802 and 806 that the monks fled to Ireland.

A beautiful Scottish casket, stolen by a Viking raiding party and carried back to Scandinavia

Some Viking crews reached the Scottish mainland and settled there to farm the land. Some sent for their families to join them, while others intermarried with the local people called the Picts, and the Scots, an Irish tribe that had settled in Scotland in the 6th century. With time, people began to forget their different origins. Eventually even the royal families of Scotland and Norway were joined by marriage.

The Isle of Man

The Isle of Man's geographical position in the Irish Sea made it a valuable base for Viking warriors. On the island, archaeologists have found the grave of a chieftain buried in a boat with his weapons.

One legend describes how a Norwegian chieftain called Godred Crovan arrived in 1066, after fleeing from the Battle of Stamford Bridge (see page 46). He became ruler of the Isle of Man, the Hebrides and other islands, on behalf of the King of Norway.

Wales

In the 9th century, Norwegian raiding parties attacked Wales, burning, looting and raping. During one raid on Anglesey in 987, over 2,000 people were taken as slaves. Viking warriors attacked the city of St David's, sacking its cathedral and killing the bishop and most of the town's inhabitants.

Some Vikings settled in Wales and were gradually accepted by the native Welsh. Viking traders gave Scandinavian names to areas off the Welsh coast; some are still used today, such as Steephom, Skokhom and Flatholm.

Vikings arrive on the Welsh coast.

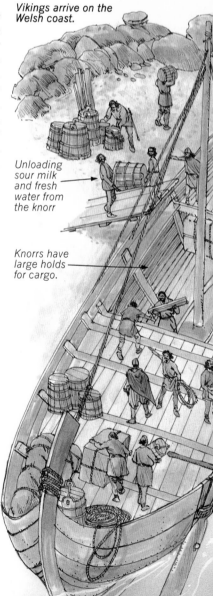

Unloading sour milk and fresh water from the knorr

Knorrs have large holds for cargo.

Ireland

In the 8th century, Ireland was a very prosperous country. It was divided into several kingdoms, but the kings were united under one leader called the High King.

Irish monasteries had become the focus of learning and of great wealth and were a good target for the Vikings. Raiders first appeared in the 790s, and carried out swift, vicious raids on isolated coastal villages and monasteries.

The Tara brooch and the Ardagh chalice are fine pieces of Irish workmanship.

In 839, the Vikings came in larger numbers. Norwegian fleets arrived and the warriors built fortified camps where they spent the winter. These camps, called long-phorts, grew into Ireland's first cities. Dublin, Wexford, Waterford and Cork all began as long-phorts.

Merchants from all over the Viking world came to buy and sell goods at the long-phorts, bringing wealth to Ireland. The Vikings built Scandinavian-style houses and craftsmen made goods influenced by Norse tastes. Many Norwegians married Irish women and settled in the towns or became farmers.

The Irish fight back

The Irish tried many times to drive out the Viking intruders. Their chance came at the end of the 10th century, when the Viking leaders in Dublin began to devote their strength and resources to gaining control of York, England. These efforts greatly weakened their position in Ireland and enabled the Irish kings to defeat them at the Battle of Tara in 960.

Loom

Barley seed

Cattle provided milk and meat.

In bad weather, tents were errected on board.

Brian Boru

In 1014, the High King Brian Boru encouraged the Irish to fight the Vikings at the Battle of Clontarf. The Irish were victorious and, after the battle, many of theNorwegians living in Dublin were massacred. But those who survived were allowed to stay in the long-phorts, because Viking trade was attracting wealth to the country.

Brian Boru was later killed by a Viking warrior while he was praying before the Battle of Clontarf.

Hidden treasure

Hoards of treasure have been found all over the Viking world. Many were hidden for safe-keeping by Norse warriors and merchants who died before they could reclaim their valuables.

Some rich treasures have been found on sites the Vikings looted. They were probably hidden by local inhabitants in haste as longships appeared on the horizon. A collection of Pictish treasure was found under the floor of a church on Shetland. Its position had been marked with a cross on the slab of stone covering it. Another vast hoard was found at Cuerdale, in Ireland, in a lead chest buried in a river bank.

Most hoards consist of jewellery, bars of precious metals and coins.

Mainland Europe under attack

The trading towns which had developed in western Europe at the end of the 8th century became the target of Viking attacks in the 9th century. Without adequate military organization, Europe was unable to deal with the raiders. Apart from their own bodyguards, the fighting men available to local lords were usually poorly-armed peasants. They were no match for Viking warriors, who stole horses from coastal villages and made lightning attacks across the countryside.

Charlemagne and the Frankish empire

One of the most prosperous kingdoms in 8th century Europe was that of the Franks. It was ruled by Charlemagne, a powerful emperor, who successfully conquered large areas of Europe.

Charlemagne was an excellent military leader, with a well-equipped and efficiently organized army. During his reign, Vikings had little success raiding Frankish territory. He was also a patron of learning and of the arts. He encouraged poets, historians and other writers.

After Charlemagne's death in 814, the Frankish empire was divided between his descendants. But they fought each other instead of defending the empire. As a result, Viking raiders were more successful. They plundered the trading town of Dorestad in 834, and looted towns and cities, such as Rouen, Garonne, Quentowic and Paris. In 845, a fleet of several hundred longships sacked Hamburg.

A golden bust of Charlemagne decorated with precious stones

Island camps

A Viking army camping on an island

In 843, a Viking raiding party remained on the European mainland through winter instead of returning to Scandinavia. They set up camp on the island of Noirmoutier, at the mouth of a river on the Atlantic coast of France. The advantage of island camps was that attackers could be killed while trying to cross the water. Soon other Viking forces followed this example.

Longship

Tents

Campfire

The Vikings are laughing at their enemies.

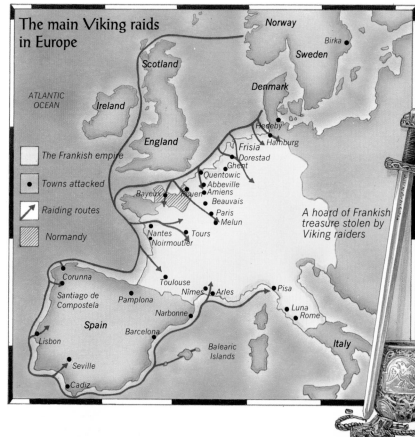

The main Viking raids in Europe

Norway
Birka
Sweden
Scotland
Denmark
ATLANTIC OCEAN
Ireland
Hedeby
Hamburg
England
Frisia
Dorestad
Ghent
Quentowic
Abbeville
Bayeux
Rouen
Amiens
Beauvais
Paris
Melun

The Frankish empire

• Towns attacked

↗ Raiding routes

Normandy

Nantes
Tours
Noirmoutier

Corunna
Toulouse
Nîmes
Arles
Pisa
Santiago de Compostela
Pamplona
Luna
Rome
Narbonne
Spain
Barcelona
Balearic Islands
Italy
Lisbon
Seville
Cadiz

A hoard of Frankish treasure stolen by Viking raiders

The Frankish army cannot reach the Vikings.

Into the Mediterranean Sea

Viking fleets sailed as far as Spain and into the Mediterranean Sea. One such expedition was undertaken by a fleet of 62 longships and was led by two Viking chieftains, Björn Ironside and Halstein.

The attacks they launched on towns in southern Spain were largely unsuccessful. Much of Spain had been conquered by Muslim Moors from North Africa in the 8th century, and they were strong enough to repel the Viking looters. But the fleet sailed on, launching surprise attacks on coastal settlements in southern Spain. They attacked the North African coast, taking treasure and as many slaves as possible. Ironside and Halstein spent the winter on an island at the mouth of the River Rhone, before sailing to Italy.

Halstein's men fighting Muslim Moors

Halstein's trickery

One saga describes how Halstein attacked the city of Luna, in Italy, thinking it was Rome. When his men were beaten back by the city's defenders, Halstein resorted to trickery. He pretended he was dying and sent for a local priest to baptize him. His coffin was carried to the cemetery by his body-guard. Once inside the city walls, Halstein leapt out of the coffin and he and his men looted the city.

Halstein leaping from his coffin

Attempts to buy off the Vikings

European leaders desperately tried to halt the destruction caused by the Vikings. Charles the Bald, King of the Western Frankish Kingdom, tried paying 3,000kg (7,000 pounds) of silver to stop a Viking band from sacking Paris in 845. This was the first of a series of thirteen bribes paid by Frankish kings. But soon after a payment had been made, the Vikings returned and demanded further, larger bribes.

In 857, a Viking leader called Björn Ironside and his army were encamped on an island in the Seine. Charles the Bald attempted to hire a Viking force led by a man called Weland to kill Ironside and his men. But Ironside was rich with treasure stolen from Paris, and he simply paid Weland to leave his men in peace. The two chieftains joined forces and ruthlessly plundered the Seine valley.

Rollo and Normandy

Some European leaders tried to buy the Vikings' cooperation by giving them land to settle in. In 911, the Frankish king, Charles the Simple, gave the city of Rouen and its surrounding lands to a Viking leader called Rollo. In return, Rollo swore allegiance to Charles and became a Christian. One story suggests that Rollo, a proud Norseman, refused to kiss Charles' foot, which was the custom when swearing loyalty to the king. Instead, he lifted Charles' foot to his mouth and sent the king tumbling backwards.

Rollo and his men adopted the French language and soon became absorbed into the French way of life. Rollo's land was known as *Terra Normannorum*, Latin for "the land of the Northmen". We call it Normandy.

Rollo welcomed by the Archbishop of Rouen

Europe fights back

In the second half of the 9th century, the kings and leaders of Europe began to strengthen their governments and organize the protection of their lands. The Franks built fortified castles which could resist attack and serve as barracks for efficient cavalry (soldiers on horseback) and well-equipped armies. As a result, Viking invasions were less successful.

Paris was savagely attacked and sacked by Vikings in 845, 857 and 865. But by the time the city came under attack again in 885, it had been fortified with stone walls. The city was besieged for ten months by a Viking fleet. 30,000 Viking warriors launched repeated assaults, but the 200 French soldiers inside the fortress held out until the Vikings withdrew. Paris proved that the Vikings could be beaten if towns were properly defended.

The Vikings reach America

Using the Shetland Islands and the Faroes as stepping stones, Vikings from Norway and Denmark sailed westward across the Atlantic Ocean, searching for new land to colonize and farm. They entered uncharted seas, not knowing whether or not they would find land. Some ships and their crews were lost in storms and sea mists, before settlers reached Iceland and Greenland.

The search for new lands continued and during their frequent journeys west, Viking adventurers became the first Europeans to reach America. Leif Ericsson, a Norwegian adventurer, set foot in America 400 years before Christopher Columbus set sail.

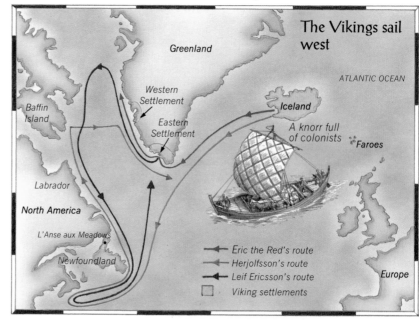

The Vikings sail west

Vikings in Iceland

Legends attribute the discovery of Iceland to three different men. The first man to reach the island was a Norwegian sailor called Naddod, who found it when his ship was blown off course in about 860.

Early explorers were followed by colonists, most of whom came from Norway, but some were Vikings who had settled in Ireland. The climate in the south of Iceland was similar to that in parts of their homeland, and the settlers were able to farm a variety of crops and cattle. Regular trading relations were maintained with Scandinavia and mainland Europe.

Eric the Red settles on Greenland

Greenland was discovered in about 900 by a man called Gunnbjörn. While sailing from Norway to Iceland, a ferocious storm blew

his ship toward an unknown island, which he called "Skerries".

The most famous Viking to explore Greenland was a Norwegian known as Eric the Red because of his red hair and fiery temper. Sagas say Eric was involved in "some killings" in Norway and fled to Iceland to escape punishment. But he committed murders on the island too, and was exiled from Iceland for three years.

Eric spent this time exploring Skerries. It was not a very fertile place, yet Eric called it "Green Land", hoping the name would encourage people to go there.

This is a page from a manuscript which tells the story of Eric the Red discovering Greenland.

In 985, he set off from Iceland with 25 cargo ships that were full of colonists, their possessions and livestock. Only 14 ships reached Greenland. The others were either destroyed by great waves and storms, or were forced to turn back to Iceland.

A boat of hunters killing whales

Hunters used spears and bows and arrows to kill their prey.

A merchant ship arriving

Vikings who settled on Iceland and Greenland hunted walrus, seals and whales.

Life on Greenland

Eric and his followers settled on the southwest coast of Greenland. Their colony became known as the Eastern Settlement. The Western Settlement, an area 320 kilometres (200 miles) northwest of Eric's land, was colonized by another party of Vikings some years later.

The climate in Greenland was slightly milder in Eric the Red's time than it is today. The settlers were able to grow barley and to raise sheep, goats and cattle on the limited pasture land. They exported the ivory tusks of walruses and of small whales called narwhals. They sold falcons, the furs of arctic foxes and the skins of polar bears. Metals, timber and some grain had to be imported by merchant ships from Scandinavia or Europe. Vikings remained on Greenland for 400 years. But, after the 12th century, the climate grew colder. Settlers were attacked by Inuits (islanders from the north of Greenland) who had been driven south by harsh weather. Finally, disease, cold and lack of food killed most of the settlers. Only a few returned to Iceland.

Inuits still live and hunt in Greenland today.

Vikings sight America

In 985, Bjarni Herjolfsson set sail from Iceland to join his father on Greenland. His boat was blown off course and became lost in fog. When visibility improved, Herjolfsson realized that the thickly forested coastline he could see was not Greenland. When he finally reached Greenland, he told people what he had found. Experts now think that Herjolfsson had sighted America.

Leif Ericsson

In about 1000, Leif Ericsson, son of Eric the Red, became the first European to land in America. He retraced Herjolfsson's route and landed in three places on the east coast of America. Leif gave these places names: Helluland, meaning "rock land", probably after the landscape of what is now Baffin Island; Markland, which means "forest land", which is thought to be an area in Labrador; and Vinland, which means "land of grapes". Vinland is believed to be either part of New England or Newfoundland.

A statue of Leif Ericsson in Reykjavik, Iceland

Leif spent the winter in Vinland before returning to Greenland. They had sailed a total of about 11,000 kilometres (about 7,000 miles). Leif's brother, Thorvald, took a party of settlers to Vinland and lived in the houses built by Leif's crew. They were attacked by native Americans, who they called Skraelings, meaning "wretches". Thorvald was killed and the survivors fled home to Greenland.

This is what a Skraeling might have looked like.

More colonists come

Members of Eric the Red's family made two more expeditions to Vinland. The first included the widow of Leif Ericsson's brother Thorstein (who had been killed trying to recover Thorvald's body). At first the settlers traded successfully with the Skraelings. But relations deteriorated and, after two years, the colonists returned empty-handed to Iceland.

The second expedition was led by Leif's sister Freydis. Again feuds with the Skraelings forced the party to flee. Vinland proved to be too remote for the Vikings to colonize. Communications and supplies could not be relied on, and the Skraelings were far too numerous and hostile to overcome.

Evidence and fakes

For many years archaeologists suspected that the Vikings had reached America. But the only evidence that was produced, such as a map of the northeast coast of America said to date from Viking times, turned out to be a fake.

The Kensington Stone

In 1898, a farmer from Kensington, Minnesota in the USA, produced a stone carved with runes*. He claimed to have found the stone, now known as the Kensington Stone, in the roots of a tree on his land. But experts proved that the runes were not genuine. Some people even suspected that the farmer had carved them himself, copying them from a book found in his house.

But in 1968, the remains of several Viking-style buildings and other objects were discovered in L'Anse aux Meadows, Newfoundland.

Wooden remains

Sailing East

In the 7th century, groups of Swedish warrior-merchants began to sail east, across the Baltic Sea, to conquer and trade. By the 8th century, they were sailing up rivers into eastern Europe.

At first the Vikings pillaged the native Slavs. But later they settled, and Swedish chieftains became rulers of Slav cities, such as Novgorod and Kiev. The Slavs called the Vikings "Rus" and the area in which the Rus settled is now called Russia.

Ibn Fadlan, an Arab diplomat, met a group of Rus merchants on his travels. He described them as "tall as date palms, with blond hair and ruddy complexions".

Trading posts

Rus merchants established trading posts at the mouths of the rivers which flowed into the Baltic Sea. During winter, Vikings sheltered in these settlements and pillaged the surrounding area. In spring, they began to row their cargo-laden boats inland. They sailed in fleets for protection. These fleets were sometimes as large as a hundred boats and carried the largest volume of trade in Europe at that the time

River journeys

Lake Ladoga was the starting point of two possible river routes into Russia. Some Viking merchants sailed east along the River Volga to the town

The Vikings' routes east

— The Vikings' routes east

···· Portage stages

A Rus merchant

of Bulgar or the port of Itil. These trading towns were situated on overland routes to the East and the Far East. Arab silver could be obtained there in exchange for furs and slaves. Farther south, across the Caspian Sea, the Rus reached the markets of Baghdad.

Other groups of Vikings sailed south from Lake Ladoga, down the River Dnieper, and across the Black Sea to Constantinople. It was a dangerous journey, with seven sets of rapids on the river between Kiev and the Black Sea. The rapids could only be passed during a few weeks of high water each year.

Viking boats were sailed and sometimes rowed along the Russian rivers. When moving from one river to another, or avoiding rapids, the crews had to carry their boats or roll them along the ground using logs. Moving a boat in this way is called "portage". It was exhausting work and the Vikings often used Slav slaves to help them.

These men are using logs to move their knorr. While on land, the Vikings were vulnerable to ambushes by tribes of Slavs.

The Slavs

Before the arrival of the Vikings, Russia was populated by a people called the Slavs. They were hunters and farmers who had developed trading posts where they sold the goods they produced. Their peace had been disrupted by the arrival of Germanic tribes* and Magyars (horse-men from the East).

A Slavic earring found in Scandinavia

Rurik the Rus

In the 8th century, Slav tribes in Russia were troubled by internal fighting. It is said that in a desperate attempt to bring peace, they invited three Rus brothers to rule them in c.860. Soon after this, one of them, called Rurik, seized his brothers' lands and created a new kingdom based around the city of Novgorod.

Oleg the Wise

Rurik was succeeded by his relative, Oleg, known as "the Wise". Oleg won the allegiance of Slavs around Novgorod and expanded the area under his control as far south as Kiev, which he seized in 882. This enlarged territory was known as the kingdom of Kiev.

After his death, Oleg's successors continued to rule over the Slav tribes in the kingdom of Kiev and they established lucrative trading contacts with Constantinople.

Vladimir the Saint

Vladimir became leader of the kingdom of Kiev in 978, after two of his brothers had died in a struggle for the throne. He is known as "the Saint", despite legends which say he kept 800 concubines* and slave girls in his palace.

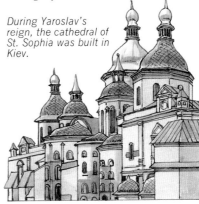

Vladimir was a very shrewd politician and a fine diplomat. When he wanted to establish close trading ties with Constantinople, he sent a group of warriors to Emperor Basil II to act as his bodyguard. They later became known as the Varangian Guard (see page 43).

Vladimir of Kiev

In return, Vladimir signed a trade alliance with Constantinople, which was sealed by his marriage to the Emperor's sister, Princess Anna. Emperor Basil agreed to the marriage on condition that Vladimir became a follower of the Christian Church.

In 988, Vladimir was baptized and forced his subjects to follow his example. A mass baptism was carried out by Byzantine priests and churches were built throughout Russia. Vladimir was later made a saint for converting so many people to the Christian faith.

Vladimir's citizens were baptized in the River Dnieper by Byzantine priests. Rus warriors forced people into the water.

Yaroslav the Wise

After Vladimir's death, his sons fought each other for the crown of Kiev. Three of them were killed before a fourth, Yaroslav, finally managed to seize control. During Yaroslav's reign, Kiev reached the peak of its power. Learning and literature flourished, law and order was established and trade with Constantinople prospered.

Yaroslav's successful reign is also reflected in the international marriages he was able to arrange for himself and members of his family. He married a Swedish princess, strengthening his ties with Scandinavia, and ensured that his daughters married into the royal families of Norway, France and Hungary.

During Yaroslav's reign, the cathedral of St. Sophia was built in Kiev.

The decline of Kiev

The descendants of Rurik the Rus ruled Russia until 1591. But after 1054, the power of the kingdom of Kiev began to diminish. Bickering between Yaroslav's sons, and repeated attacks from a tribe from Asia called the Polovtsy, weakened the kingdom and caused a decline in its prosperity.

Constantinople: "the Great City"

Constantinople (now called Istanbul) was the capital of the eastern half of the Roman Empire (later known as the Byzantine empire). Its geographical position made it a very important market for trade between Europe and Asia. Parties of Vikings journeyed there across the Black Sea. Many were merchants, attracted by the exotic luxury goods available at the city's markets. Others were mercenaries, hired to fight for the Byzantine emperor.

The Great City

The Vikings called Constantinople *"Miklagard"*, which means "the Great City". In the 9th century, it was the richest, most powerful city in Europe. At a time when most cities had populations of only a few thousand, Constantinople had about one million inhabitants.

Constantinople had inherited the magnificence of the Roman Empire, but had also developed its own sophisticated culture. Byzantine art was characterized by its rich hues, geometric designs and very stylized figures. Pictures made of small pieces of pottery tile, glass, metal and precious stones, called mosaics, were very popular.

The court of Constantinople was known for its magnificence, its

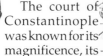
A Byzantine empress

elegant, wealthy courtiers and spectacular ceremonies. Behind the scenes, however, it was rife with intrigues, plots and conspiracies involving nobles fighting for political power. Several emperors died violently, stabbed, poisoned, blinded or strangled. One empress even blinded her son to prevent him from succeeding her. Those courtiers whose intrigues failed were sometimes murdered or imprisoned in monasteries.

Vikings attack the city

The Northmen were so impressed by the wealth of Constantinople that they were strongly tempted to attempt to capture it. In the 9th and 10th centuries, Rus chieftains launched several assaults on the city. In 907, Oleg the Wise, Prince of Kiev, sent a fleet of 2,000 longships carrying 80,000 men.

The Rus attacks were defeated because their fleets were destroyed by "Greek Fire", which was a mixture of chemicals whose formula was known only by the Byzantines. It burned fiercely on water and was difficult to put out.

The Emperor of Constantinople receives Olga, a Rus queen, and her embassy in the Byzantine court.

Viking merchants visit

After their unsuccessful attempts to conquer Constantinople, the Vikings concentrated on setting up trading contracts with the city. Many merchants arrived there, with cargoes of furs, slaves, swords, wax, amber, walrus ivory and honey to trade. In exchange, they purchased luxury goods, such as silks from China and India, gold and silver coins from Arabia, and other goods, such as glass, bronze and silver vessels, beads and fine glazed pottery.

A Varangian Guardsman in dress uniform

Wealthy women of the court

Wealthy Rus ambassadors

Queen Olga

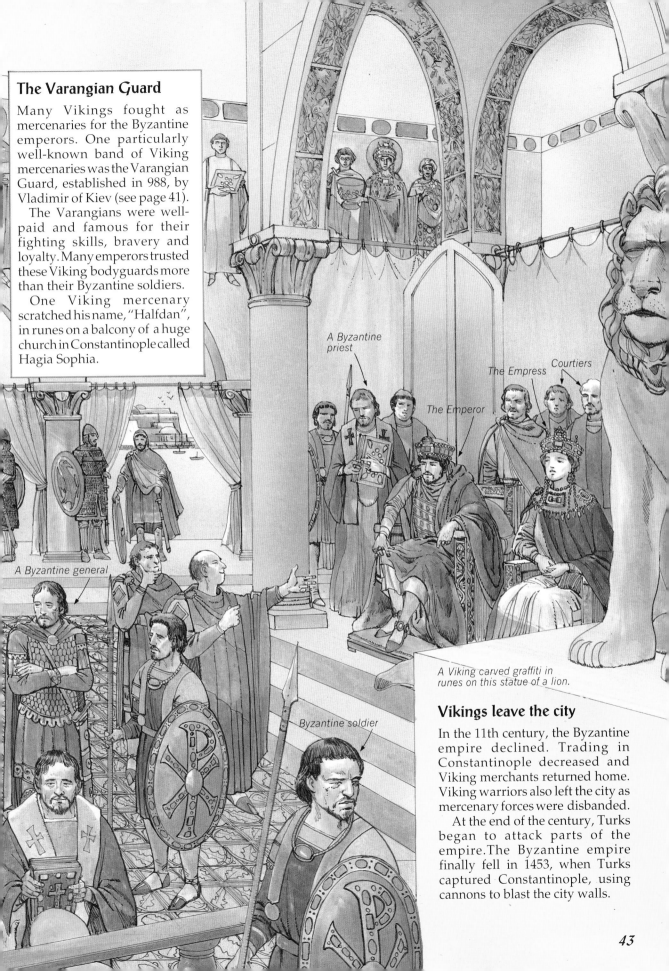

The Varangian Guard

Many Vikings fought as mercenaries for the Byzantine emperors. One particularly well-known band of Viking mercenaries was the Varangian Guard, established in 988, by Vladimir of Kiev (see page 41).

The Varangians were well-paid and famous for their fighting skills, bravery and loyalty. Many emperors trusted these Viking bodyguards more than their Byzantine soldiers.

One Viking mercenary scratched his name, "Halfdan", in runes on a balcony of a huge church in Constantinople called Hagia Sophia.

A Byzantine priest

The Empress

Courtiers

The Emperor

A Byzantine general

Byzantine soldier

A Viking carved graffiti in runes on this statue of a lion.

Vikings leave the city

In the 11th century, the Byzantine empire declined. Trading in Constantinople decreased and Viking merchants returned home. Viking warriors also left the city as mercenary forces were disbanded.

At the end of the century, Turks began to attack parts of the empire. The Byzantine empire finally fell in 1453, when Turks captured Constantinople, using cannons to blast the city walls.

Islam and its empire

During the Viking Age, Arab culture was flourishing. In the 9th century, the empire conquered by Arab warriors stretched from the frontiers of India, across the Middle East and North Africa, to Spain. The empire was united by a common religion, called Islam, which had been founded in the 6th century by the Prophet Muhammed.

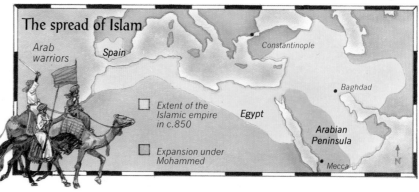

The spread of Islam

Arab warriors

Spain

Constantinople

Baghdad

☐ Extent of the Islamic empire in c.850

Egypt

Arabian Peninsula

☐ Expansion under Mohammed

Mecca

N

Muhammed and Islam

Muhammed (c.570-632) was a wealthy merchant who taught that there was only one god, called Allah. By the time Muhammed died, his teachings were accepted throughout Arabia.

After Muhammed's death, his followers, known as Muslims, were ruled by a series of elected leaders called caliphs. The caliphs were completely dedicated to spreading Islam and their armies rapidly conquered new territory.

In the mid 7th century, the Islamic empire began to split. Rival dynasties struggled for power when the followers of Islam divided into two sects: the Sunni and the Shi'ites.

The wealth of the East

The Islamic empire continued to flourish and expand in the 8th century. Silver from mines near Samarkand and Tashkent in Central Asia made the caliphs fantastically rich. The wealth and magnificence of the caliphs' court in Baghdad is described in a book called *Tales of One Thousand and One Nights*.

Baghdad was one of the most sophisticated cities in the Muslim world and was the site of great intellectual achievements. When the Arab conquerors overran the provinces which had been under Roman and Byzantine control, they gained access to the learning of the classical world. Using this and their own knowledge, Arab doctors, mathematicians and astronomers of this period were far more advanced than their counterparts in Europe.

Astronomers in an Islamic illustration

Seamen

The Arabs were experienced seamen, whose skills were as impressive as those of the Vikings. Arab merchants regularly sailed to markets in East Africa, India and China.

Arab sailors used a selection of navigational instruments. These included astrolabes (used to estimate local time by measuring the Sun's altitude), compasses (invented by the Chinese), and water clocks.

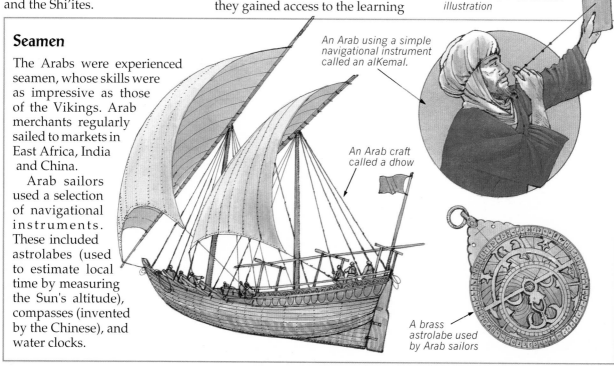

An Arab using a simple navigational instrument called an alKemal.

An Arab craft called a dhow

A brass astrolabe used by Arab sailors

A camel train taking goods from Persia and China going to markets in the Middle East.

Muslim explorers

Muslim explorers set out on great journeys seeking knowledge of the world beyond their empire. In 943, an explorer called Ibn Haukal began an expedition that was to last over 25 years. He reached West Africa and saw the Sahara Desert and the River Niger.

Some Arabs journeyed north across the Caspian Sea into Russia. One diplomat called Ibn Fadlan went up the River Volga in 921 and met a group of Rus merchants. Cleanliness and hygiene were very important to the Muslims, and in a written account of his travels, Ibn Fadlan notes that the Rus were the "filthiest of God's creatures". You can read more about Ibn Fadlan and the Rus on page 22.

This picture shows a busy market in the East, where merchants from Scandinavia, China and India have come to trade.

Vikings in Arab lands

Viking merchants made their way to markets in Baghdad, Itil and Samarkand to trade with the Arabs. Like the Byzantines and the Slavs, the Arabs called the Northmen "Rus".

The Vikings offered ivory, swords, amber, fur and slaves. In exchange, they wanted silver coins which they could melt down to make ornaments or use at home as currency. They also wanted luxury items like herbs, spices and precious stones from India, silk from China and ornaments made of glass and silver.

To encourage their customers to accept them, some Viking merchants adopted the fashions of the countries they visited. For example, some wore baggy trousers gathered at the knee, which were Eastern in style. The remains of a coat which is decorated with horizontal bands and fastened with a row of buttons down the chest, have been found at Birka, in Sweden. Buttons were rarely used on Viking clothes, so experts think the garment was inspired by costumes seen in the East.

The end of Arab silver

Between 800 and 965, Viking towns such as Birka and Hedeby thrived, as a huge number of silver coins came flooding into the country. Altogether about 85,000 Arab silver coins have been found in Scandinavia.

The supply of silver decreased rapidly after 965 and had stopped altogether by the beginning of the 11th century. This was probably caused by shortage in the mines themselves. The end of Arab silver had a disastrous effect on Hedeby and Birka, which were deserted in 975.

Arab coins

A spice seller

Swords

Rus traders selling slaves

A Viking trader wearing Eastern style trousers

Silk cloth

This Viking merchant is exchanging amber beads for cloth

A Rus trader wearing a jacket like the one found in a grave at Birka

This is a bronze Arabian charcoal burner found in Sweden.

A bronze figure of Buddha from India, found in Scandinavia

The last Viking expeditions

During the 11th century, the Viking Age drew to an end. Viking raids became less successful, as Europe's leaders assembled well-equipped armies, fortified their cities, and built castles from which they could defend their territory.

If there is one date which marks the end of the Viking Age, it is 1066. During this year there were two invasions of England, which could be called the last major Viking expeditions. The first was by Vikings from Norway, and the second by the Normans, Vikings who had settled in France (see page 37). Scenes of the Norman invasion taken from the Bayeux Tapestry*, appear in the long panels at the top and bottom of these two pages.

Norman soldiers outside a well-fortified castle

Three men claim the English throne

In 1066, Edward the Confessor, King of England, died without a son. The heir to the English throne, Edgar the Athling, was only a boy. So a council of nobles and churchmen gave the crown to Harold Godwinsson, the Earl of Wessex. But two other men also wanted the English throne: Harald Hardrada, the King of Norway, and William, Duke of Normandy.

Harold Godwinsson's coronation shown in the Bayeux Tapestry

Harald Hardrada, "the last Viking"

Harald Hardrada became King of Norway in 1047. When he heard of the death of Edward the Confessor, he took a huge fleet and attempted to seize the English throne. In September 1066, he landed in the north of England, and joined forces with Earl Tostig, (Godwinsson's brother).

King Harold took the English army to meet the Norwegian invaders. They clashed at the Battle of Stamford Bridge, in Yorkshire, on the 25th of September, 1066. The Norwegians were defeated and Harald Hardrada died fighting.

Harald is sometimes known as "the last Viking", because his life as a warrior, mercenary and an adventurer is typical of many people's idea of a Viking hero.

A reconstruction of the Battle of Stamford Bridge

The Anglo-Saxons slaughtering the Viking army

Harald's bodyguards form a human shield around him.

Harald Hardrada

The Normans build their fleet and sail toward the south coast of England.

William the Norman

The Normans were descendants of the band of Vikings who settled in Normandy in the 10th century. William, Duke of Normandy, was directly descended from their leader Rollo the Ganger.

William was not related to the English royal family; his claim to the throne was based on a promise made by Edward the Confessor. Edward had lived in Normandy during a period of exile from England. He and Duke William became friends and Edward had promised to ensure that William succeeded him.

In 1064, the Earl of Wessex, Harold Godwinsson, had been forced to stay at William's court after being shipwrecked off the Norman coast. William threatened to detain Harold unless he swore to support his claim to the English throne. Harold promised reluctantly and sailed home. But Harold had not realized that holy relics were

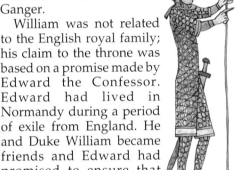

William the Conqueror

hidden beneath the altar on which he swore and this made his promise a sacred oath.

When Edward died, Harold accepted the English crown, thus breaking his oath. This prompted William to take England by force. He assembled a fleet of 700 ships and an estimated 10,000 men, including many bowmen and the best trained and equipped cavalry in Europe.

The army landed in the south of England three days after Harald Hardrada's invasion in the north. King Harold was still celebrating his victory over Hardrada's army when news came of William's arrival. He and his men hurried south to meet the Normans at the Battle of Hastings. The exhausted Anglo-Saxons were beaten after eight hours of fierce fighting and King Harold was killed. William, who later became known as "the Conqueror", was crowned the new King of England.

Normans in Italy

While William of Normandy was conquering England, another group of his Norman subjects were busy conquering part of Italy. At this time southern Italy was controlled by Byzantines and Arabs. The Normans were led by Robert Guiscard and his brother Roger. Robert conquered an area in southern Italy called Apulia, and took the title Duke of Apulia.

Roger seized the island of Sicily. One of his descendants, Roger II, became the King of Sicily in 1130. He set up a magnificent court at the heart of Mediterranean Europe, achieving a goal their Viking ancestors had failed to achieve.

This mosaic shows Roger II being crowned King of Sicily.

The end of the Viking Age

Viking raids did not completely stop after 1066, but they were much rarer. The last raid on England was in 1151, and the Scots repelled a Norwegian attack in 1263. Scandinavian merchants continued trading throughout Europe. Scandinavia itself had become increasingly stable and peaceful. Its kings united and established firm control over their countries and colonies. Farming, crafts and trade flourished and the spread of Christianity throughout Scandinavia led to a new outlook, with people rejecting the old ways. The vitality and energy that had characterized the Vikings slowly died away, only surviving in sagas and legends.

A 10th century pendant

The Norman cavalry and bowmen fought the Anglo-Saxons at the Battle of Hastings.

The world at the time of the Vikings

The Vikings

700s

c.780 The Vikings launch their first raids on mainland Europe.

Raids on England and on mainland Europe become increasingly frequent.

The hilt of a highly decorated Viking sword

800s

c.850 Viking explorers discover Iceland.

Swedes visit Russia and attack Constantinople.

900s

920 Greenland is sighted.

Vikings trade with Baghdad and Constantinople.

Vikings settle in Normandy.

Viking coins

1000s

980 The Irish defeat Vikings at the Battle of Tara.

Leif Ericsson reaches North America.

1013 Sweyn Forkbeard of Denmark becomes King of England and is succeeded by his son Cnut.

1047 Harald Hardrada is crowned King of Norway.

1066 Harald Hardrada and Normans invade England.

1100s

c.1100 The Viking Age is over.

China

618-907 The T'ang dynasty rules China. Art and literature enjoy a "golden age". At its height, the T'ang dynasty rules the largest empire of its time.

China imports horses, precious stones, ivory, gold and furs, and exports tea, paper, lacquer, silk and ceramics by boat and along a trade route called "the Silk Road". Confucian philosophy and Taoist religion are popular, as well as Buddhism (from India).

A Chinese dragon design decorated everything belonging to the Emperor.

907 The T'ang dynasty ends and China is divided by civil war.

960 The Sung dynasty (960-1279) comes to power in China. New inventions include mechanical clocks, paper-making, earthquake detectors, umbrellas, gunpowder and fireworks and magnetic compasses. The first printed book is produced in 868.

Books were printed using wooden stamps.

The Chinese invented gunpowder and used it to make fireworks.

Japan

794 The Japanese Emperor rules from Heian (Kyoto). His people believe he is a descendant of the Sun Goddess and therefore sacred. This period of Japanese history is called the Heian period. Powerful families gradually take over power and rule on behalf of the emperor.

852 The Fujiwara family controls the Japanese emperor and the government until 1160.

A lute inlaid with mother of pearl, made in the 8th century

The Japanese adapt Chinese script to develop their own system of writing.

Buddhism and Confucianism are studied and the Chinese Civil Service and arts are imitated.

The Phoenix Hall, Uji, near Kyoto, erected in 1053 during the Heian

1050 Warriors called Samurai emerge in Japan. They fight for the nobles in return for land and wealth. As the Fujiwara family's control declines, the rival Minamoto and Taira clans compete for control of the government. Samurai take part in this feud.

A Japanese Samurai warrior in 18th century leather armour

Africa

780 Arab traders visit West Africa to buy slaves and huge quantities of gold. Chinese and Arab merchants trade with East Africa. Camel trains cross the Sahara to great trading cities which grow up there. A powerful trading empire develops in Ghana.

800 The kingdom of Kanem Bornu in West Africa develops into a great empire.

Arab traders negotiating for gold with an African king

900 The empire of Ghana becomes fabulously rich. Arab visitors write about the large towns, fine houses and many beautiful women.

909 The Muslim Fatamid dynasty controls north Africa until 1072. The Fatamids conquer Egypt in 969.

Camel caravans crossing the Sahara desert

1030 The Muslim Almoravids dynasty controls Ghana, north Africa and Spain.

1100 The Kingdom of Ife in Nigeria rises to power.

Middle America

800 The Classical phase of Mayan civilization (based in central America) ends, probably due to wars between rival kings and overcultivation of the land.

The Maya had built great cities of stone, with palaces, open plazas, courts for a special ball game, and stepped pyramids with temples on top.

The Maya had a very complicated calender, and a system of writing which scholars are only just beginning to translate.

900 Yucatan becomes the new focus of Mayan culture during the Post Classical Period.

c.920 Toltec warriors invade Mayan territory in the Valley of Mexico and coastal areas.

980 The Mayan city Chichen is renamed Chichen Itza by the Toltecs.

A statue of a Toltec warrior

A step pyramid at Chichen Itza

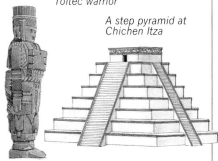

The Toltecs build their capital city at Tula.

1040 In Peru, South America, the Chimu people create a coastal empire with large towns. The Moche and Nasca civilizations also begin to flourish in Peru.

1100 The city of Tula is destroyed by tribes from the north.

A Peruvian warrior depicted on a pottery vase

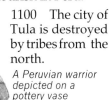

India

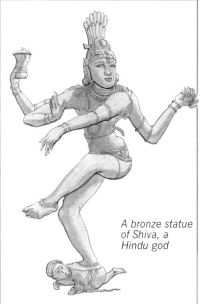

A bronze statue of Shiva, a Hindu god

900 India becomes a wealthy nation, attracting merchants and conquerors. Arab merchants visit regularly.

Buddhism spreads from India to Japan and China. It loses its popularity in India, to be replaced by Hinduism.

920 Indian kingdoms break up into many different states. The Rajput people dominate central and northern India.

985 Rajara I rules the Chola kingdom in southern India.

997 Mahmud, Sultan of Ghazni (now Turkestan) conquers an empire in northern India and in eastern Afghanistan.

Muktesvara Temple, Bhuvanesvara, India, built in the 10th century

Norse legends

The Vikings told many stories about their gods and goddesses. Below are some of the most important ones. You can read more about some of the Norse gods and goddesses and the places that appear in these legends on pages 24 and 25.

Odin's wisdom

More than anything else, Odin wanted to possess great knowledge and understanding. So he went to a place in the underworld called Jotunheim, to search for the Fountain of Knowledge. He found it guarded by a god called Mimir. Odin asked if he could take a drink from the fountain. Mimir agreed, but said that first Odin must pay for it with one of his eyes. Odin accepted this and from that day had only one eye.

Soon Odin wanted even more knowledge. For this he had to pay a much greater price; he had to sacrifice his life. He hung from a branch of Yggdrasil, the World-Tree, with a spear in his side for nine days and nights until he was dead. That is how he learned about the mysteries of death.

Odin used his supernatural powers to bring himself back to life. He used the knowledge he had gained to help both the gods and ordinary people. Odin also brought the runes back from the Land of the Dead and gave them to the Vikings on Midgard*.

Idunn and the golden apples

One day Odin and two gods called Loki and Honir were exploring Midgard. They grew very hungry, so Loki killed an ox. The other gods built a fire and set the meat to roast, but it would not cook.

Suddenly the gods heard someone laughing at them. The voice came from an eagle in the branches of a tree above them. The eagle boasted that he was preventing the meat from cooking. He promised to remove his spell if the gods allowed him to eat his fill of the ox

first. The gods were so hungry that they agreed and the eagle gobbled up the meat, leaving just the bones.

This made Loki furious and he picked up a staff and attacked the eagle. It grabbed the staff and flew off with Loki still dangling from the end, held there by magic. The eagle dragged Loki through thorn bushes and over rocks and glaciers. Loki begged it to stop, promising to do anything if the eagle would let him go. The eagle (who was really the giant Thiazzi in disguise) made Loki promise that before the week was over he would lure the goddess Idunn and her golden apples out of Asgard. Idunn's magic apples were supposed to keep the Norse gods eternally young.

Loki devised a plan to trick Idunn into leaving Asgard. He told her he had found a tree in Midgard that bore fruit just like her golden apples. He persuaded her to go and look at them. He suggested that she take her apples along to compare them with the new ones. As soon as Idunn set foot outside Asgard, Thiazzi (disguised as the eagle) swooped down and carried her off to his cave in the mountains of Jotunheim.

Gradually, without the magic apples to eat, the gods began to grow old and feeble. They did not know where Idunn had gone and became desperate to find her. The god Heimdall remembered he had seen Idunn leaving Asgard with Loki. The gods seized Loki and demanded to know what trickery he had been up to. When Loki eventually confessed his scheme, the gods threatened to kill him unless he bought Idunn and her apples back home to Asgard.

The goddess Freya lent Loki a magic falcon skin that enabled him to fly to Thiazzi's cave where Idunn was imprisoned. Loki flew off to Jotunheim. When he found Idunn, he changed her into a nut so that he could carry her in his beak. But as Loki set off back to Asgard, Thiazzi saw him, changed

back into an eagle and began to race after him.

The gods could see the eagle chasing Loki. Quickly, they built a fire by the wall which surrounded Asgard. As soon as Loki had flown safely into Asgard, they lit the fire and Thiazzi, who plunged after Loki, was burned by the flames. Even though the gods were now weak and feeble, they managed to kill the eagle. Idunn, who had been changed back into her proper shape, quickly gave the gods some golden apples, so restoring their youth and beauty.

The theft of Thor's hammer

Thor's most famous weapon was a double-headed hammer called Mjollnir. It always hit its target and flew back to his hand. One morning he woke to find Mjollnir had been stolen from his bedside by Thrym, a Frost Giant. Thor swore he would take revenge.

Thrym said he would return the hammer if Freya agreed to become his wife. But Freya refused angrily and so a plan was needed. Thor dressed up like a bride, pretending to be Freya, and Loki pretended to be her bridesmaid. Together they set out for Thrym's hall.

When they arrived, the wedding feast began. Thor almost gave the game away by indulging his huge appetite for food and drink. But Loki quickly explained to the guests that the bride had not eaten for days because she was so excited about getting married. This delighted Thrym and, in accord with tradition, Mjollnir was brought out for bride and groom to swear their vows on. The moment he saw his precious hammer, Thor threw off his veil, and grabbed Mjollnir. He and Loki killed Thrym and several of the wedding guests.

Loki's brood

Against Odin's solemn orders, Loki took an evil giantess as his mistress. She gave birth to three monstrous children: Fenrir, a giant wolf, Jormungand, a serpent, and

Hel, who was half a beautiful woman and half corpse.

The gods were furious at Loki's disobedience. They had been warned that his monstrous children could bring disaster. So they threw Jormungand into the Ocean which surrounded Midgard and banished Hel to Niflheim in the underworld (where she became Queen of the Dead). Fenrir, the wolf, was only a cub and seemed harmless, so the gods let him wander about freely in Asgard.

But Fenrir grew so huge and fierce that the gods had to find a way of restraining him. First, they pretended that they needed him to test the strength of a chain. They tied it around him, hoping that he would be unable to break it. But Fenrir broke the chain. The gods tried again with an even stronger chain, but the wolf broke it easily.

The gods sent a servant to the Dwarfs' workshop, offering them a huge reward if they could make a chain that was strong enough to bind Fenrir. The Dwarfs produced a silken ribbon which was magic and could not be broken. But when the gods asked Fenrir to test the ribbon, he became suspicious. He said he would only agree to be bound with the ribbon if he could have a god's hand in his mouth, to prove they were not tricking him. The god Tyr agreed.

The wolf was tied with the ribbon and tried to free himself. The more he strained, the tighter the ribbon became. Finally, Fenrir demanded to be released. When the gods refused, he crashed his jaws together, biting off Tyr's hand. The gods dragged Fenrir into an underground cave and tied him to a rock where he could do no harm.

The death of Balder

Balder, son of Odin and his wife, Frigg, was greatly loved by all the gods. But one night he had a dream about his own death. Odin grew worried and galloped to Niflheim,

where he consulted the ghost of a prophetess. She told him that Balder would die and that nothing could be done to save him.

Frigg would not accept her son's fate. She made every dangerous thing in the universe swear not to wound him. Soon the gods were playing a new game. Anything they threw at Balder would veer away leaving him untouched.

But Loki was terribly jealous of Balder's popularity and wanted to harm him. He disguised himself as an old woman and went to Frigg's hall. He found out that only the mistletoe plant had failed to promise not to harm Balder. Loki made a dart from mistletoe. Then he joined in the gods' game. He persuaded Balder's blind brother, Hoder, to throw the mistletoe dart at Balder. Loki guided his hand. The dart pierced Balder's heart and killed him.

In despair, Frigg sent her son Hermod to Niflheim to beg for Balder's return. Hermod was told that if everyone and everything in the universe wept for Balder, he would be allowed to return to Asgard. Hermod rushed back with the good news. Everything wept for Balder, except one evil giantess, who refused to shed a tear. So Balder had to stay in the Land of the Dead. The giantess was Loki in disguise and he smiled at what he had done.

Loki's punishment

The gods realized that Loki was responsible for the death of Balder. After he had mocked them at a feast, they decided it was time for him to be punished. Loki fled, pursued by the gods. He changed himself into a salmon and hid in a waterfall, but the gods knew his tricks and caught him in a net.

The gods wanted Loki to suffer for his crimes. They turned one of his sons, called Vali, into a wolf which tore his other son, Narvi, to pieces. Then they took Loki to a cave deep in the mountains and tied him across some sharp rocks.

Above him was a great snake, wound around the stalactites on the roof, dripping poison from its fangs. The poison burned Loki's face.

Loki's faithful wife, Sigyn, sat beside her husband, protecting him by catching the snake's venom in a bowl. But while she turned to empty the bowl, the poison fell on Loki, making him scream in agony.

The end of the world

The Vikings believed that the downfall of the gods and the end of the world would be caused by a last great battle called Ragnarok. Ragnarok means "the doom of the Gods". Nobody knew exactly when Ragnorak would take place. But according to some predictions, it would be at a time when there was constant fighting between the gods and giants, and when wars on earth caused people to turn on their own families and kill them. Loki and Fenrir the wolf would finally break free from their chains. They would be joined by Hel, Jormungand and giants and creatures from the underworld. Together they would attack Asgard. A great battle would rage until almost all the gods had been killed and Loki's army had perished.

After Ragnarok, Midgard would freeze. All the human beings would be killed except for one pair who would climb into the branches of Yggdrasil for shelter. The sun and the moon would be eaten by two terrible wolves and the light of the stars would be extinguished, leaving the world in complete darkness and chaos.

After the destruction, the Vikings believed that Balder and his wife would rise from the dead, bringing Hoder and Vali with them. The surviving gods would start a new race of gods. The two surviving humans who had hidden in the branches of Yggdrasil would climb down from the tree and begin to repopulate the earth. In this new world, everyone would live in peace and harmony.

Key dates in the Viking Age

500/800 Waves of barbarian immigrants from Asia and the Steppes arrive in Europe after the collapse of the western Roman Empire.

789 Three Viking ships raid Dorset in southwest England.

793 Vikings raid the monastery on Lindisfarne in England.

794 A monastery at Jarrow, on the northeast coast of England, is attacked by Vikings

795 Raids begin on the Scottish island of Iona and on Ireland.

799 Viking ships raid southwest France.

800 The Vikings build permanent camps on the islands of Orkney and Shetland.

Charlemagne is crowned as emperor.

810 Danish Vikings raid Frisia.

814 Charlemagne dies and his empire declines.

830 Raids on the British Isles and the Frankish empire become more frequent and vicious.

c.830 Swedish Vikings sail east and begin trading with towns around the Baltic.

834 Dorestad in Frisia is raided.

841 The Vikings build the first long-phort at Dublin in Ireland.

843 Viking raiders stay over winter on an island camp in the mouth of a river at Noirmoutier, on the west coast of France.

844 The Vikings sail to Spain but the Arabs repel their attacks.

845 Ragnar Hairy Breeches besieges Paris. As a result, the first Danegeld* is paid to tempt the Vikings to leave.

Vikings raid Hamburg.

c.850 The Oseberg ship is buried.

850/1 Danes raiding England camp on the Isle of Sheppey in the River Thames, and stay over winter for the first time.

Swedish Vikings begin to explore Russia.

851 Norwegian Vikings are expelled from Dublin, but seize control of the city again later the same year.

859 Björn Ironside launches a raiding expedition to Spain and the Mediterranean Sea.

860 Rurik the Rus establishes a kingdom based in Novgorod, Russia.

Vikings discover Iceland.

The first Viking attack on Constantinople is made by a Swedish fleet.

c.860 The Gokstad ship* is buried.

Vikings raid North Africa and Italy.

862 Vikings settle in Kiev and Novgorod in Russia and begin to trade with Constantinople and Baghdad.

866 The Danes' "Great Army" lands in England.

867 The Great Army captures York.

871 Alfred the Great becomes King of Wessex.

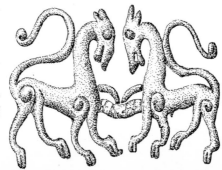

874 Vikings settle on Iceland.

A trading treaty between the Rus and the Byzantines is established.

878 Vikings in England are beaten at the Battle of Edington by Alfred the Great.

Swedish Vikings in Russia set up trading towns at Novgorod and Kiev.

885 Paris is besieged by a huge fleet of Viking ships, but manages to resist attack.

886 The Danelaw* is established in England.

c.900 Harald Finehair becomes the first king of all Norway.

907 Oleg the Wise sends a fleet to attack Constantinople.

911 Normandy is given to the Viking leader Rollo.

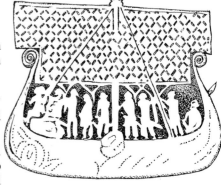

936 Gorm the Old becomes the first king of all Denmark.

941 Igor of Kiev sends a fleet to attack Constantinople.

945 Harald Blue-Tooth becomes King of Denmark.

954 Eric Bloodaxe is expelled from York in England, and killed.

c.960 King Harald Blue-Tooth of Denmark is converted to the Christian faith.

974 The German Emperor Otto II seizes Hedeby in Denmark.

978 Ethelred the Unready is crowned King of England.

Vladimir the Saint becomes the ruler of the kingdom of Kiev.

980 The Irish defeat the Vikings at the Battle of Tara.

Harald Blue-Tooth builds royal fortresses at Trelleborg and Fyrkat.

c.980s Viking raids on England are renewed.

983/6 Eric the Red explores and later colonizes Greenland.

986 Bjarni Herjolfsson sights Vinland.

987 Sweyn Forkbeard becomes King of Denmark.

988 The Varangian Guard is established in Constantinople by Vladimir of Kiev.

Vladimir forces his people in Kievan Russia to become Christian.

c.990 England and France pay bribes called Danegeld to raiding parties to avoid being plundered.

995 Olaf Tryggvason becomes King of Norway.

Olof Skötkonung becomes King of Sweden.

1000 Christianity is adopted as the official religion in Iceland.

1002 Massacre of St Brice's Day in England.

Leif Ericsson reaches Vinland

1008 King Olof of Sweden is converted to Christianity.

1009 Olaf the Stout attacks London and pulls down London Bridge.

1013 Sweyn Forkbeard conquers England but dies soon after. He is succeeded by his son Cnut. Danes rule England until 1042.

1014 Brian Boru defeats Vikings at the Battle of Clontarf.

Cnut becomes King of Denmark.

1015 Olaf Haraldsson seizes the Norwegian throne.

Yaroslav the Wise becomes Prince of Kiev.

1019 Yaroslav becomes leader of Kievan Russia.

1028 Olaf Haraldsson, King of Norway, and the King of Sweden wage war on Cnut of Denmark.

1030 Cnut defeats and kills Olaf Haraldsson at the Battle of Stiklestad. He becomes King of Norway, Denmark and England.

1042 Sweyn Estridsson becomes King of Denmark.

Edward the Confessor is crowned King of England.

1047 Harald Hardrada becomes King of Norway.

1066 Edward the Confessor dies without an heir.

Harold Godwinsson is crowned King of England.

Harald Hardrada invades England but is defeated and killed at the Battle of Stamford Bridge.

Duke William of Normandy invades southern England and defeats Harold Godwinson at the Battle of Hastings. William (known as the Conqueror) becomes King of England.

1075/80 Adam of Bremen writes his history of the Vikings.

1096 The first Crusade* is launched.

1100 The Viking Age comes to an end.

The pictures on this page are designs found on Viking rune stones or jewellery.

The Viking World map

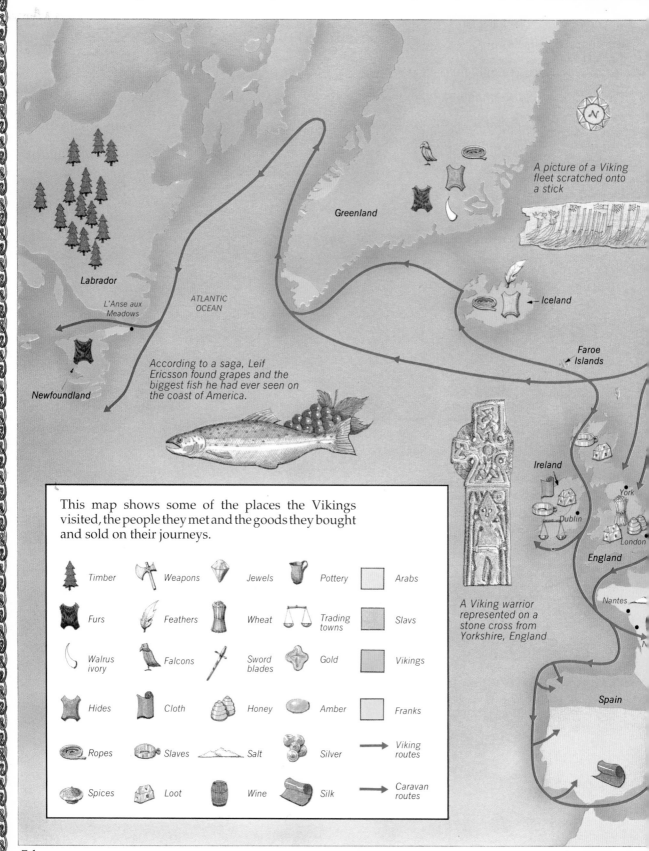

Greenland

Labrador

ATLANTIC
OCEAN

L'Anse aux
Meadows

Newfoundland

According to a saga, Leif
Ericsson found grapes and the
biggest fish he had ever seen on
the coast of America.

A picture of a Viking
fleet scratched onto
a stick

←— Iceland

Faroe
Islands

Ireland

Dublin

York

London

England

A Viking warrior
represented on a
stone cross from
Yorkshire, England

Nantes

Spain

This map shows some of the places the Vikings
visited, the people they met and the goods they bought
and sold on their journeys.

Timber		Weapons		Jewels		Pottery		Arabs
Furs		Feathers		Wheat		Trading towns		Slavs
Walrus ivory		Falcons		Sword blades		Gold		Vikings
Hides		Cloth		Honey		Amber		Franks
Ropes		Slaves		Salt		Silver		→— Viking routes
Spices		Loot		Wine		Silk		→— Caravan routes

The Vikings called the ocean "the whale's road"

This is a woodcut print of a group of Vikings carrying their boat. This is called portage.

Tashkent

Samarkand

Bulgar

Novgorod

Sweden

Birka

Kiev

nark

eby

rg

CASPIAN SEA

BLACK SEA

Arab coins

Italy

Constantinople

Baghdad

Rome

Jerusalem

Alexandria

MEDITERRANEAN
SEA

Sicily

A set of merchant's scales found
in a grave at Birka, Sweden

North Africa

Who was who in Viking times

This section gives details about the lives and deeds of some of the most important people who lived during the Viking Age. If a name is in **bold** text, that person also has his or her own entry in this list.

Adam of Bremen (c.1076). German canon from the Cathedral at Hamburg. He wrote *The Deeds of the Archbishops of Hamburg*, which contains valuable information about Scandinavia and the Vikings.

Alcuin of York (735-804). Anglo-Saxon monk and a famous scholar. He was invited to **Charlemagne**'s palace at Aix-la-Chappelle, where he became the chief adviser on education and religion. He founded a school in the palace and helped to develop Charlemagne's ideas about the role of a king.

Alfred [the Great] (849-99). Anglo-Saxon King of Wessex from 871. After many defeats, he saved Wessex from Danish invaders by signing a treaty that allowed them to settle in East Anglia. He reformed his army and his country's government. He built ships and towns and encouraged learning and the arts.

Anna Comnena (1083-1148). Daughter of the Byzantine Emperor Alexius I and wife to the Emperor Nicephorus Bryennius. After her husband's death, she entered a convent and wrote *The Alexiad*, a history of her father's reign, which is considered an important source of information on this period.

Queen Asa. 9th century Queen of Norway. She was the grandmother of **Harald Finehair**. Some stories say she murdered her husband and went unpunished. Experts think that she was buried on the magnificent Oseberg burial ship.

Athelstan (c.895-939). Anglo-Saxon King of Wessex and Mercia from 925. An outstanding warrior, he was the grandson of **Alfred the Great**. In 926, he was acknowledged as king of all the English and invaded Wales and Scotland. In 937, at the Battle of Brunanburgh, he defeated the Danes of York.

Björn Ironside. 9th century Viking leader and son of **Ragnar Lodbrok.** He led the Viking army that sacked Paris in 857. **Charles the Bald** hired a group of Vikings, to attack Björn, who was besieged with his men on the Isle of Oissel, in the River Seine. Björn bought off Weland with some of the loot he had stolen from Paris.

He led 62 ships on one of the greatest expeditions during the Viking Age. Driven from the coast of Spain, by Muslim forces, Björn's fleet crossed to Morocco and looted coastal areas. He took many prisoners as slaves. His fleet then sailed on, raiding Spain, France and Italy. It is said he even reached Alexandria, Egypt. In 861, his fleet was defeated near Gibraltar, but they managed to sail on and at Pamplona, Spain, they captured the prince and were paid a huge ransom.

Brian Boru (941-1014). High King of Ireland from 1004. He was the son of a minor chief in the Irish kingdom of Munster. He dedicated his life to ridding Ireland of Viking invaders. He helped his brother, Mahoun, to become King of Munster. Together they beat the Danes at the Battle of Solloghead.

Brian fought the Danes and rival Irish chiefs to become King of Munster when his brother died in 984. He devoted himself to encouraging culture and learning.

When war broke out again, he defeated the Vikings and drove a chieftain called Sigtrygg Silk Beard from Dublin. In 1004, all the chiefs and kings submitted to Brian's leadership and he became High King of Ireland. In 1012, rebellion broke out and Brian was killed fighting the Vikings again at the Battle of Clontarf.

Charles I [Charlemagne] (742-814). King of the Franks from 768. His name means "Charles the Great". He spent many years spreading Christianity to nearby kingdoms and conquered large areas of land. He built a palace for himself at Aix-la-Chappelle and invited famous scholars to his court to encourage learning.

Charles invaded Italy and was crowned King of the Lombards. He spent many years conquering the Saxons of Germany, and forcing them to become Christians. He also fought the Muslims in Spain. In 800, the Pope crowned him Emperor of the Romans.

Charles II [Charles the Bald] (823-77). King of France from 840 and Frankish Emperor from 875. He was **Charlemagne**'s grandson. During his reign, there were constant rebellions from within his empire and from Viking invaders.

Charles III [Charles the Fat] (839-88). King of Germany from 876 and Frankish Emperor from 881. He was unable to repel Viking raids and was known for his cowardice. He paid a Viking leader called **Siegfried** a large sum of money to stop terrorizing Paris. As a result of this action, Charles was deposed. After his reign the Frankish empire was weak and disorganized.

Charles III [Charles the Simple] (879-929). King of France from 898. He gave **Rollo** control of Normandy in 911. In 923, he was deposed by Hugh the Great and fled to England where he died.

Cnut Sweynsson [Cnut the Great] (1014-1035). King of Denmark from 1018, King of England from 1016 and son of **Sweyn Forkbeard**. Cnut brought peace and prosperity to England during his reign. One well known story describes how his foolish courtiers flattered him, saying he could do anything. They believed he could control the sea; but he tried and failed.

Edward the Confessor (1003-66). King of England. The Danes seized the English throne from

Edward's father **Ethelred II**. Edward spent a long period of exile in Normandy. When he returned to England to be crowned king in 1042, he preferred Norman courtiers and styles. He built a magnificent abbey at Westminster. He was a very religious man and, in 1161, he was made a saint.

Emma of Normandy (?-1052). Queen of England and daughter of Duke Richard I of Normandy. She married **Ethelred II** and was the mother of his son, **Edward the Confessor**. Later she married **Cnut Sweynsson**, with whom she had another son, Harthacnut. When Cnut died in 1035, Emma tried to put Harthacnut on the throne of England. It took her five years to achieve this, but he died only two years later.

Eric Bloodaxe (?-954). King of Norway. He killed many of his half-brothers to gain the throne. This made him unpopular and when **Harald Finehair** claimed the throne nobody supported Eric.

He fled Norway and became the king of the Viking kingdom of York. In 948, the Anglo-Saxons expelled him from York and he was killed in an ambush at Stainmore, Yorkshire.

Ethelred II [Ethelred the Unready] (965-1016). King of England from 978. His nickname means "the ill advised". He was crowned king after his mother murdered his half-brother. During his reign, Ethelred unsuccessfully tried to buy off Viking invaders. He ordered the Massacre of St Brice's Day in 1002. When **Sweyn Forkbeard** invaded England in 1013, Ethelred fled to France. He returned in 1016, but was defeated by Sweyn's son, **Cnut**.

Earl Godwin (?-1053). Anglo-Saxon appointed Earl of Wessex by King **Cnut** of England. He helped **Edward the Confessor** come to the English throne in 1042. Edward married Godwin's daughter, Edith. Godwin and his sons virtually ran the kingdom. They were opposed

to Edward's Norman advisers and courtiers. Banished in 1051, they returned to England in 1052, and the family was reinstated.

Gormflaith of Leinster. 10th century Irish princess. Her first husband was Olaf Kvaran, a Danish King of York. When he died, she married the Irish High King, Mael Seachlainn, but he divorced her. She then married **Brian Boru,** to seal a peace between Boru and her brother, the King of Leinster. When her brother sided with the Danes against Brian in 1012, Gormflaith fled to join her son Sigtrygg Silk Beard, the Danish King of Dublin. It is said that Sigurd, Jarl of the Orkneys, agreed to help the Danes if he was allowed to marry Gormflaith, but he was killed during the fighting.

Harald Finehair (c.850-930). King of Norway from 860. Members of his family ruled Norway until the 11th century. Between 866 and 872, he fought to impose his rule over other chieftains in Norway. Some left the country rather than accept his rule. In 890, he led a successful expedition to capture the Orkneys, Shetlands and Faroes. He had at least 20 sons, who fought each other for the throne when he died.

Harald Gormsson [Harald Blue-Tooth] (c.910-985). First king of all Denmark from 950. He became a Christian and made Christianity Denmark's official religion. He built royal fortresses at Trelleborg and Fyrkat (see page 30). He was deposed in 986 by his own son, **Sweyn Forkbeard**, and died soon after in exile.

Harald Sigurdsson [Harald Hardrada] (1015-1066). King of Norway. His nickname means "the hard ruler" or "the ruthless". At the age of 15, he supported his half brother, Olaf Haraldsson, at the Battle of Stiklestad. He was wounded and hid in a farmhouse to recover. As soon as he could

travel, he was smuggled to Sweden and then Kiev. He had many adventures in the service of Prince **Yaroslav the Wise**, whose daughter, Elizabeth, he married. He served in the Varangian Guard of the Emperor of Byzantium.

Harald returned to Norway in 1045 and seized the throne when his nephew Magnus I died in 1047. He was killed attempting to invade England in 1066.

Harold II [Harold Godwinsson] (c.1022-1066). King of England from January to October 1066. He was a powerful Earl of East Anglia and Essex and became the Earl of Wessex when his father, **Earl Godwin,** died. He promised to support **Duke William of Normandy**'s claim to the English throne, but when **Edward the Confessor** died, Harold accepted the crown himself. Harold was killed at the Battle of Hastings by the invading Normans.

Harun el Rashid (766-809). Caliph of the Abbasid dynasty from 786. There are many legends about the magnificence and prosperity of Harun's court in Baghdad. In an attempt to gain an ally against the Byzantines and his Muslim rivals, he sent presents and ambassadors to **Charlemagne**. One gift is said to have been two elephants.

Ibn Fadlan. 10th century Arab diplomat. He was the secretary to an embassy from the Caliph of Baghdad that visited the region of the Middle Volga (Russia) in 921. He wrote a detailed account of the Rus and of the funeral of a chieftain that he witnessed.

Odo of Neustria. 9th century Frankish leader. In 885, Odo and his men defended Paris which was besieged by Vikings. Odo and a few followers escaped through enemy lines. They reached **Charles the Fat,** who began to raise an army. Odo returned to Paris and held out till Charles' army arrived. After Charles was deposed, Odo became the Count of Paris. He was crowned and was a powerful king. His descendants ruled France for many generations.

Olaf Haraldsson [*Olaf the Stout*] (?-1030). King of Norway from 1014. Before he came to the throne, he spent 12 years as a "professional Viking". He raided in the Baltic and attacked towns in northern Europe.

In 1009, he was sailing up the River Thames raiding, and found his path blocked by London Bridge. Olaf sailed under the bridge and tied ropes around its wooden supports. He and his men then rowed off downstream, pulling the bridge apart.

Olaf served in Normandy, where he was converted to Christianity in 1014. When he became King of Norway he used brute force to convert his subjects.

Olaf was exiled from his throne and died trying to regain his kingdom at the Battle of Stiklestad. After his death, Olaf was declared a saint.

Olaf Tryggvason [*Olaf the Saint*] (c.965-1000). King of Norway from 995. He was the great-grandson of **Harald Finehair**. Many legends were written about his heroic adventures.

When his father King Trygve was murdered, Olaf fled to Russia. He spent time serving under **Sweyn Forkbeard**. Olaf became a Christian while raiding England in 994. When he became King of Norway he introduced the Christian faith there. He was defeated by a combined Danish and Swedish fleet at the Battle of Svold in 1000. He is said to have leapt overboard when he realized the battle was lost.

Olga (c.890-968). Princess of Kiev and the wife of Igor the Wise. She ruled Kiev while her son, **Syvatoslav**, was too young to become king. She visited Constantinople in 957. While she was in the city, she was baptized and became a Christian. When she returned to Kiev, she tried to spread Christianity among her subjects. After her death she was made a saint.

Emperor Otto I [*Otto the Great*] (912-973). King of Germany from 936. In 962, he became the first person to be crowned Emperor of the Holy Roman Empire. At the Battle of Lechfeld in 955, he ended the threat posed by the Magyars.

Ragnar Lodbrok [*Ragnar Hairy Breeches*]. 9th century Viking chief. His nickname referred to the trousers his wife made for him. The breeches were made of thick fur, boiled in pitch and rolled in sand to make them resistant to a dragon's fiery breath.

Ragnar raided England, but he was taken prisoner by the King of Northumbria. He was thrown into a pit of snakes, where he died.

Robert I [*Robert the Devil*] (?-1035). Duke of Normandy from 1026. He was a direct descendant of **Rollo**. He kept firm control of the Norman barons and was a powerful but unpopular ruler, as his name "the Devil" suggests. Robert was the father of **William the Conqueror**.

Rollo the Ganger (c.860-927). Viking chieftain. Rollo was called the Ganger (meaning "the walker") because he was so large no horse could carry him. He had to go everywhere by foot.

Outlawed for stealing cattle in Norway, he began raiding France and invaded much of Normandy. Desperate to make peace, **Charles III** allowed Rollo to hold the land he had overrun. In 911, Rollo was converted to Christianity.

Siegfried. 9th century Viking military leader. He led a fleet of 700 ships and 40,000 Vikings up the Seine, France, in 885. They were planning to raid the rich land of Burgundy in eastern France. When the fleet reached Paris they found the city fortified, and **Odo of Neustria** and 200 French knights refused to let the Vikings pass.

Siegfried and his men lay siege to Paris, using battering rams and huge wooden constructions to try and pierce the city walls. They floated burning longships toward the wooden fortifications but the wind blew them away from their target. When Charles the Fat and his army arrived to relieve the Parisian garrison, he paid Siegfried 320 kg (700 lb)) of silver to go away.

Sweyn Forkbeard (986-1014). King of Denmark and of England. He seized the Danish throne from his father, **Harald Blue-Tooth**. He led a successful invasion of England in 1013, and was crowned king, but died after five weeks on the throne.

Syvatoslav (957-73). King of Kiev. He was the son of Igor the Wise and his wife **Olga**, and came to the throne of Kiev as a child. Syvatoslav was a skilled warrior who overthrew the Khazars and fought the Bulgars and the Byzantines.

While making their way along the River Dneiper, he and his men were ambushed by a tribe of hostile Slavs called Patzinaks. Syvatoslav was killed and his skull made into a silver mounted drinking cup.

Theofano (942-91). Byzantine princess. She married the Holy Roman Emperor, Otto II. A keen patron of art, learning and religion, her court became the focus of cultural activity. When her husband died in 983, she looked after the throne until her son, Otto III, was old enough to rule.

William the Conqueror (1027-1087). Duke of Normandy from 1035 and King of England from 1066. William was the illegitimate son of **Robert I**, Duke of Normandy. He married his cousin, Matilda of Flanders, who was descended from **Alfred the Great**. He was a friend and distant relative of **Edward the Confessor**. When Edward died, William claimed the English crown, which he won at the Battle of Hastings in 1066.

Yaroslav the Wise (1014-1054). Prince of Kiev from 1036 to 1054. He fought his brothers to gain the throne. He made the Church of St. Sophia in Kiev into an important academy of learning.

The Scandinavian kings

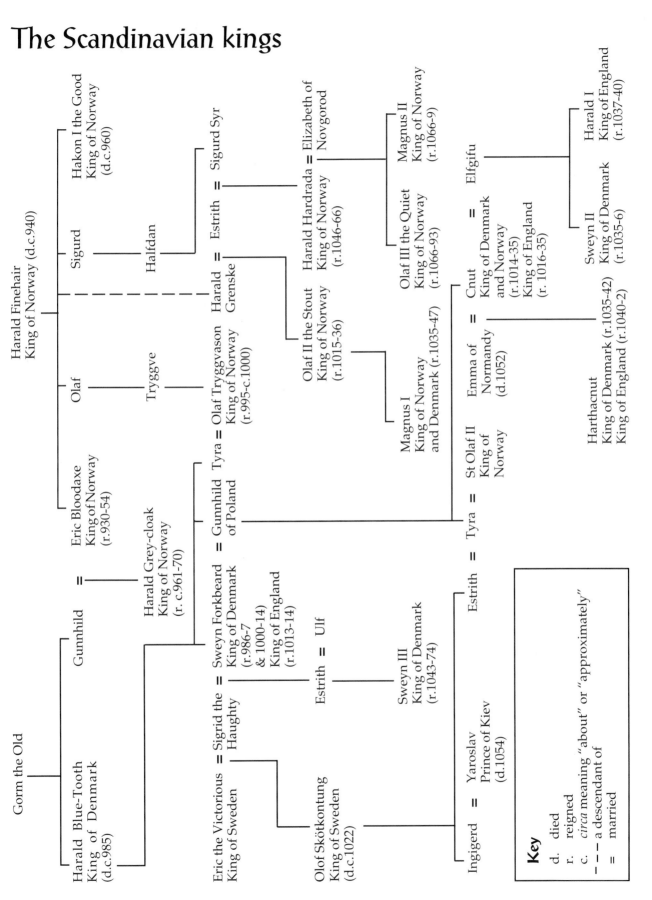

Glossary

Many Viking words used in this book are explained below. The list also includes English terms in the book that may be unfamiliar. Words used within an explanation which have their own entries in this list are in **bold** type.

Amber   The fossilized resin of pine trees. Resin is a substance that oozes from the bark of some trees. After thousands of years, it fossilizes and becomes hard, shiny and yellow.

Amulets   Lucky charms which people carried in the hope that they would bring good luck or keep away evil. Amulets were made in the shape of sacred objects or small figures of gods. A popular amulet in Viking times was in the shape of Thor's hammer.

Arab   A native inhabitant of a peninsula in the Middle East called Arabia. The Arabs conquered large areas of land in the 7th and 8th centuries. The name "Arab" is also used as a general term to describe the people living within that empire and sharing its culture and the Islamic faith.

Archaeologist   A person who learns about past cultures by digging up the remains of people, buildings and objects from earlier times.

Archbishopric   The area governed by an archbishop, a high ranking clergyman in the Catholic Church.

Asgard   The name given to the world in which the Vikings believed their gods and goddesses lived.

Baptism   A ceremony at which a person is immersed or sprinkled with water, as a sign that they have become a Christian.

Bayeux Tapestry   A wall-hanging 70 m (231 ft) long, embroidered with scenes depicting the events leading up to the **Norman** conquest of England in 1066.

Experts think the tapestry was commissioned by Bishop Odo, the half-brother of William the Conqueror, who wanted it to hang in the Cathedral in Bayeux, France.

Halley's Comet, which appears once every 75 years, is shown in the tapestry.

Caravan   A group of merchants, their servants and their pack animals, who travel together for safety.

Concubine   A term applied in a historical context to a woman who lives with a man without being married.

Danegeld   A sum of money paid to Viking raiders to leave a country in peace.

Danelaw   The area of northern and eastern England where Alfred the Great allowed the Vikings to settle after he had defeated them in 886.

Draught   The depth of water needed to make a boat float.

Emperor   The supreme ruler of an **empire**. Usually the kings of conquered lands are among his subjects.

Empire   A widespread area of land (usually including more than one previously independent state) united under the control and government of one ruler.

Feud   A long, bitter dispute between individuals or families. Feuds can last many years and are often very violent.

Fjord   A long, narrow inlet of the sea which runs inland between high cliffs. The coastline of Scandinavia has many fjords.

Free man or *Free woman*   A man or woman who was not owned by another person as a slave and whose parents had been free.

Germanic tribes   Germanic comes from the Latin word *Germanii*, which is the name the Romans gave to the tribes who lived east of the Rhine and north of the Danube. Some of these tribes had originally migrated from Scandinavia.

Gokstad ship   A 9th century royal ship found at Gokstad, Norway, in which a Viking king was buried.

Jarl   A wealthy person of noble birth in Viking society.

Karl   A free peasant in Viking society.

Keel   The long piece of wood which runs from one end of a ship to the other, forming the backbone of the vessel. The framework of the boat is attached to the keel.

Diagram showing the keel of a Viking ship

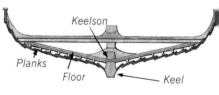
Keelson

Planks

Floor

Keel

Knorr   A cargo ship used by Viking settlers or merchants.

Long-phorts   Camps established by Vikings in Ireland. They were first used to shelter raiders in winter. The camps later developed into prosperous trading towns.

Longships (also called *dragon ships*)   Long, narrow Viking war ships used by raiding parties and in sea battles.

Mercenary   A hired soldier, paid to fight in a foreign army.

Midgard The name the Vikings gave to their world, earth.

Missionary A priest sent by the Christian Church to convert people to the Christian religion.

Norman A person descended from the Vikings who had settled in the part of France now known as Normandy at the beginning of the 10th century.

Norman soldiers depicted in the Bayeux Tapestry

Norse A word used to describe anything which relates to Scandinavia in ancient and medieval times and to the people who lived there (including the Vikings). The Vikings were known as "the people from the North" or "Northmen", and this eventually became "Norsemen".

Old Norse The language spoken by the inhabitants of Scandinavia from about 700 to 1350.

Oseberg ship A 9th century royal ship in which a Viking queen was found buried at Oseberg, Norway.

Palisade A wall constructed of strong, pointed, wooden stakes, used for protection.

Peat Decomposing plant matter which has been soaked with water. When dry can be used as fuel.

Prophetess A woman who claims to be able to foretell the future, inspired by gods and goddesses.

Ragnarok The last great battle between the **Norse** gods and the giants, which is described in Norse legends. After the battle the world comes to an end and most of the gods perish.

Roman Empire The **Romans** built up a huge **empire** in Europe and around the Mediterranean. The empire reached its greatest extent early in the 2nd century A.D. and declined in the 4th century.

Romans A people from Italy who took their name from the city of Rome. Rome was founded c.753 B.C. The cultural influences of the Romans can be seen in Europe today.

Rune A mark or letter used in the Vikings' system of writing.

Rus The name used by Slavs and **Arabs** to refer to the Swedish warrior-merchants who raided and traded in Eastern Europe, Constantinople and Baghdad. The area in which the Rus settled was named Russia after them.

Sacrifice An offering made to a god or goddess. Viking sacrifices often involved the ritual killing of both humans and animals.

Sagas Stories told by *skalds* about Viking men and women and historical events. Sagas were passed down by word of mouth until the 13th century when they were written down by scholars.

Skald A poet who composed and recited Viking poems and **sagas**.

Skraelings The name the Vikings gave to the native American Indians they encountered in **Vinland**. In Norse the word meant "wretches".

Tannery A workshop where animal skins are made into leather by soaking them in a liquid containing tannic acid and mineral salts.

Thing An open-air meeting attended by Viking **free men**, at which matters of government and law were discussed.

Thrall A Viking slave.

Valhalla The hall of the **Norse** god Odin in **Asgard**. Viking warriors who died bravely in battle were taken to Valhalla, where they feasted and fought all day.

Valkyries Handmaidens who served the **Norse** god Odin. They carried the souls of dead Viking warriors to **Valhalla**.

Odin on horseback is greeted by a Valkyrie.

Varangian Guard Viking warriors hired by the Emperor of Constantinople as his bodyguards.

Viking Age The period of Scandinavian history which started about 790 and ended about 1100.

Vinland The name Leif Ericsson gave to the area in North America where he and his crew landed. It is generally thought to be part of New England or Newfoundland.

Wattle and daub A type of wall which is made by weaving long, flexible twigs together to form a framework. This framework is then covered with a mixture of straw and mud, which dries into a hard, plaster-like covering.

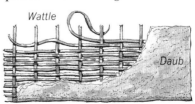

Wergeld The amount of money the Vikings considered somebody's life was worth.

Index

People who appear in the book are always entered in this index under their first names. Page numbers in italic type denote map references.

First published in 1993 by Usborne Publishing Ltd, 83-85 Saffron Hill, London EC1N 8RT, England.
First published in America March 1994
Copyright © 1993 Usborne Publishing Ltd.

Printed in Great Britain